Building and Displaying Scale Model Aircraft

with Paul Boyer

KALMBACH
BOOKS

Printed in the United States of America

97 98 99 00 01 02 03 04   9 8 7 6 5 4 3 2 1

For more information, visit our website at http://www.kalmbach.com

Publisher's Cataloging in Publication
(Provided by Quality Books, Inc.)

Boyer, Paul, 1949–
     Building and displaying scale model aircraft / with Paul Boyer.
   — 1st ed.
     p. cm.
     ISBN: 00-89024-237-2

     1. Airplanes—Models—Design and construction.   I. Title.

TL770.A2B69 1997   629.13l3'1
                                     QBI97-40655

Book and cover design: Kristi Ludwig

DEDICATION

To Dorothy, whose hobbies allow her to understand my enthusiasm for mine!

ACKNOWLEDGMENTS

Without the assistance of the following, this book would not have been possible: Bob Hayden, Marcia Stern, and Dick McNally of *FineScale Modeler;* Terry Spohn of Kalmbach Books; Andy Sperandeo and Keith Thompson of *Model Railroader;* Jim Hinds of Richmond Controls; Dana Bell of the Smithsonian Air & Space Museum; Bert Kinzey of Detail & Scale; Dave Menard of the Air Force Museum; Rich Mellilo of Floquil/Polly S Color Corp.; photographer Jim Forbes; and modelers Al Jones, Ross Whitaker, David Veres, David Balcer, Jim Mesko, and Norm Filer.

MEET PAUL BOYER

Paul has been building models since the late 1950s, and although he has built cars, tanks, and ships, aircraft are his favorite subjects. Paul served in the U.S. Air Force as a still photographer and pulled a tour of duty in Vietnam and Thailand.

Joining the staff of *FineScale Modeler* in late 1982, Paul now serves as senior editor. He writes staff features, edits freelance submissions, and oversees the Workbench Reviews and the Questions & Answers clinic in the magazine. Paul regularly attends local, regional, and national model shows, and his models are on display at the Mitchell Gallery of Flight Museum (at Milwaukee's Mitchell Airport), at the Experimental Aircraft Association Air Adventure Museum in Oshkosh, Wisconsin, and at the Smithsonian Air & Space Museum in Washington.

He and his wife, Dorothy, reside in Cedarburg, Wisconsin, north of Milwaukee. When he isn't building or writing about models, Paul likes birding, golfing, and listening to rock and jazz music. Paul hopes to complete his entire collection of more than 500 1/72 scale U.S. military aircraft kits—someday!

PROLOGUE

I hate modeling, don't you? Now, don't get me wrong—I love models. I love buying them and collecting them. I love to display them, and once in a while I enter them in competitions.

But the act of modeling—the getting there—seems to delay my gratification. Sometimes, it's frustrating. If only I could bring the box home, say "presto chango," and have it finished to perfection. Hey, it's my fantasy!

I've been building models for 40-some-odd years, and I've found that the more I build, the better I build. I've learned to anticipate hurdles and get a leg up on them before they become pitfalls. I've learned what works and what doesn't, and what I like and what I don't.

You'll probably notice after leafing through the book that each model is a 1/72 scale (1 inch equals 6 feet) U.S. military aircraft. I decided in the late 1960s that my area of interest would be the theme of my collection. The scale offers the widest range of subjects if not the greatest detail. U.S. military aircraft are the subject of countless reference books and magazines, and there are loads of museum examples to study. I've even had the chance to talk with some of the crew members of the real aircraft I've copied in miniature. So this collection offers me the best of all worlds—a subject that interests me and the availability of kits, accessories, and references that can't be beat.

As you can see, I LOVE this hobby. I just wish I could get all the models done and put them on display.

The first chapter of my book deals with the tools and materials you'll need to successfully build good-looking models. Chapters Two through Nine deal with one model each, and each one is a little more difficult than the one before. The final chapter talks about model-display ideas. After all, what good is a fine model if you are the only one to appreciate it?

Well, talking about it ain't gettin' it done, so let's start from the beginning—as good a place as any!

Paul Boyer
Cedarburg, Wisconsin

CONTENTS

1

What You'll Need to Make Model Airplanes

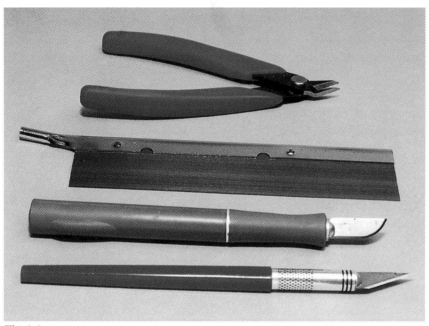
Fig. 1-1

Essential cutting tools (bottom to top): a sharp no. 11 blade with handle; a no. 10 curved blade; a razor saw; and a parts nipper.

Most of the models I build are injection-molded plastic airplane kits, just like the ones you find in hobby shops. But this hobby doesn't end there. Other types of kits, aftermarket details and accessories, paints, tools, and reference materials are available.

You won't need everything that's out there, but there are a few tools and materials you should have on your workbench.

Speaking of workbenches, you don't need anything fancy, but you should have a small table or desk where you can work and leave your project while you attend to life's other pleasures. Make sure there is plenty of light, access to electricity, and good ventilation.

The first tool you should buy is a good hobby knife (such as an X-acto no. 1 handle with no. 11 blade) (fig. 1-1). Buy replacement blades, too. I also find the no. 10 blade valuable, and it fits the same handle. Its

Fig. 1-2

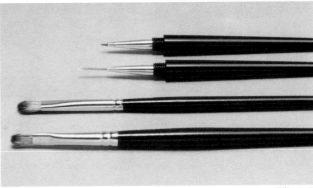
Fig. 1-3

More essentials: sanding pads (coarse, medium, fine, extra-fine, and polishing); needle files; and fine-point tweezers.

Good-quality pointed and flat bristle brushes are requisites.

curved cutting edge allows more control and works better than the straight no. 11 blade in certain situations.

Next up is a parts nipper. There are several brands; I use a Xuron to cut the injection-molded parts from the sprues.

Get a good razor saw about 1" deep with fine teeth. Zona and X-acto are among the brands available.

Keep a sharp, clean pair of scissors handy. Tweezers are important for handling small parts and decals (fig. 1-2).

As you gain experience, you'll find that filling and sanding the seams of plastic kits makes them look more realistic. I use several grits of sanding sticks (Flex-i-Pad is one brand). You can find larger examples in the nail-care section of drug stores. Also buy a set of jeweler's files.

Models look best when painted, and good-quality paint brushes are a must (fig. 1-3). I use several small round and flat brushes for painting small details, so the only large brush I have is for dusting the models.

The Most Important Tool

While the majority of beginners will paint their models with a brush, I recommend investing in an airbrush and a compressed air source (fig. 1-4). There are dozens of brands from which to

The best modeling tool (and the most expensive) is a good airbrush and compressed air source.

Fig. 1-4

Fig. 1-5

If you're going to be spraying a lot, you should invest in a good spray booth, one that draws fumes out of your work area with a powerful fan.

choose, and several methods of supplying air to the tool.

An airbrush is a miniature spray gun. Air (supplied by a compressor or other source) blows across a tiny orifice at the tip of the paint nozzle, drawing paint from the reservoir (cup or a bottle) and blowing it out in a fine, narrow mist.

Without question, the airbrush is the best way to paint models. It offers fine control and produces smooth finishes that make your model look like the real thing—and that's the whole idea.

A good airbrush and air source are going to set you back nearly $200—easily the most expensive purchase you're likely to make in this hobby. I have several airbrushes, but one air source. I use a 20-pound industrial cylinder of carbon dioxide (CO_2) for "air." It is completely silent, the regulator allows adjustment of the air pressure, and I don't have to worry about condensed water vapor building up in the air hose. The down side is that the cylinder with regulator is expensive, and every year or so, I have to haul the cylinder to a supplier to have it filled with CO_2.

If you're going to be spraying a lot, consider buying or making a spray booth (fig. 1-5). This unit will safely dump paint fumes outside your work area. Although it can be expensive, it is a worthwhile project—without adequate ventilation, glue, paint, and thinner fumes could build up to harmful levels.

Buy a set of tiny drill bits (fig. 1-6). These can be used either in a pin vise (inexpensive but slow working) or in a motor tool (expensive but fast).

A motor tool should be considered optional equipment. If you choose to add it to your tool box, buy one that connects to a separate speed control unit. You want to be able to adjust the speed of the tool to keep it from damaging the model you're working on.

Tiny drill bits can be used in a pin vise or in a motor tool.

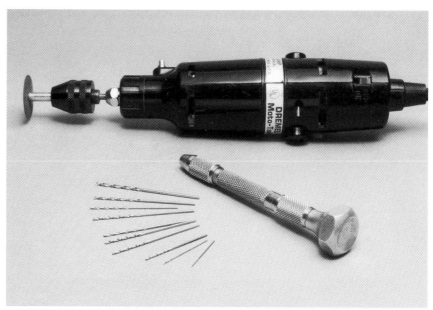

Fig. 1-6

Materials

Paints and their thinners are important purchases. Many brands are available, and you can choose from oil-base enamels or water-base acrylics. Water-base paints are certainly safer but a little more difficult to use.

These days, just about every shade ever used on military equipment has been produced in modeling paint.

Use the thinner that is made for the type of paint you're using—you'll have fewer problems. To save money, buy a quart can of lacquer thinner to clean brushes and airbrush parts.

Spray cans of paint are another way to finish your models, but they have drawbacks (see Chapter Three).

Since most models feature water-slide decals, you should obtain several brands of decal-setting solutions. Some solutions work better on some brands of decals, and some don't work at all on certain decals.

Shallow frozen-dinner trays are the ideal containers for water for decals.

Stick It to 'Em

Use liquid cement to assemble your models. Unlike old-fashioned tube glue, liquid cement is applied while the parts are held together and is allowed to run along the mating surfaces by capillary attraction. A little goes a long way. Dedicate a long-pointed brush for cementing only. I find that the little narrow-necked cement bottles are too easy to tip over, so I buy cement in pint cans and decant it into a wide-mouth glass bottle (fig. 1-7).

Fill 'er Up

A good-looking model shows no seams where the parts were glued together. Sometimes the parts don't fit well and the seams are easy to see. The answer is to fill the seams and sand them smooth.

Of the many filling materials I'm going to recommend only one—gap-filling super glue such as Zap-A-Gap. Teamed with a super-glue accelerator, gap-filling super glue can fill just about anything and be sanded as smooth as the surrounding plastic in just a few minutes.

Super glue doesn't shrink, but becomes harder when it finally cures (in a period of hours), so don't wait too long to sand. It also comes in handy for attaching parts made from dissimilar materials—resin to plastic, for example.

I usually apply gap-filling super glue by dispensing a few drops into a recycled plastic lid, then transfer tiny amounts with a toothpick.

Accelerators come in spray bottles, but they're better applied with a brush or, my favorite, a Micro Brush—a little disposable plastic stick with a

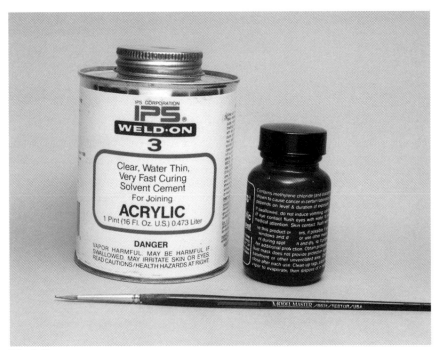

Fig. 1-7

The best glue to use on plastic kits is a liquid solvent cement. It can be purchased in large quantities and decanted into a wide-mouth jar for easy use.

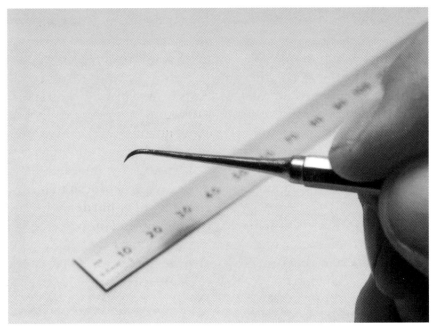

Fig. 1-8

A scribing tool and a straight-edge metal ruler can help restore or add surface detail to models.

tiny ball of fiber on the end. This holds a small drop of accelerator until you touch it to the model right next to the super glue. The accelerator runs onto the glue and sets it in seconds.

White glue, such as Elmer's Glue-All, is handy for attaching clear parts that could be damaged by solvents or super glues. It also comes in black.

Future is supposed to be a clear acrylic floor polish, but I use it as a clear gloss coat and a final coating for clear canopies.

Arm yourself with a steel scribing tool, such as the Squadron Tool shown (fig. 1-8). You'll be able to restore recessed panel lines lost in seam filling, and you can cut rapidly (and cleanly) through plastic with it.

Make sure that you have a good steel ruler. You'll use it as a

Aftermaket decals present endless possibilities for markings on most military aircraft models.

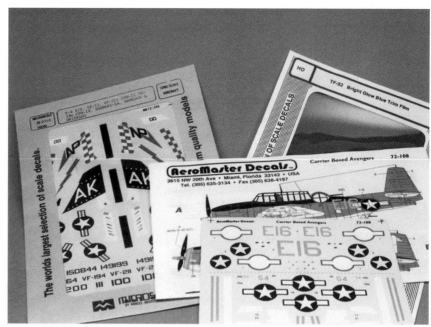

Fig. 1-9

straightedge, as well as a measuring tool.

In addition to cellophane tapes, I use drafting tape (like masking tape, but less sticky), Parafilm M (available from Testor's), and Bare-Metal Foil as masking materials. Bare-Metal Foil is a thin, self-stick, alloy foil used by car modelers to create chrome trim, but I use it to mask canopies.

Obtain a good selection of styrene sheets, strips, tubes, and rods for making new parts.

Aftermarket decals offer the option of changing the markings of your model from those supplied in the kit (fig. 1-9). There are also sheets that supply letters and numbers, and most valuable of all, solid colors that you can trim and apply to fit your model.

Artist's pastel chalks work great for weathering models. Get a starter set from an art-supply store.

Reference Materials

Perhaps the most enjoyable part of this hobby is learning about the airplane you're modeling. Hobby shops and book-stores have lots of books and magazines that will help you research your models and make them accurate.

Monographs such as Squadron/Signal's In Action and Detail & Scale series can provide more detailed information than you will ever need.

And a good modeling magazine (*FineScale Modeler*, of course) will keep you up to date on new products and techniques to help you enjoy your favorite hobby.

Now that you have everything you need, let's get busy.

2

Your First Model Airplane

Your first kit! Monogram's SnapTite F-117 Stealth Fighter is easy to put together, doesn't require paint, and looks great when finished!

With any endeavor, you don't want to start with something beyond your reach. For your first model airplane, start with something simple—a snap-together plastic kit.

Perfect for this occasion is Monogram's SnapTite F-117A Stealth in 1/72 scale (kit no. 1148). There are only 11 parts (including a two-piece stand) and peel-off, self-stick paper markings.

You won't need glue; the parts snap together and stay together. And you won't need paint; the Stealth is black, and so is the plastic used to make the kit (except for the yellow-tinted clear canopy). Best of all, the model has enough detail to satisfy even experienced modelers, and it's an accurate miniature representation of this famous warplane.

After you have rushed home with your newfound kit, take time to examine the parts and the instructions. Make sure all the parts are included. Usually,

Parts nippers are perfect for cleanly cutting plastic parts from the sprues.

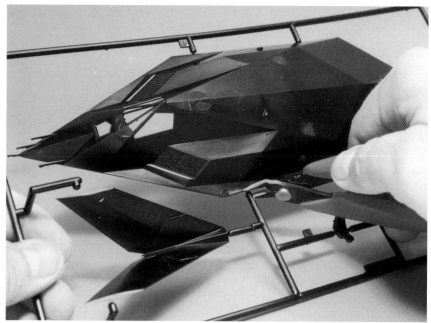

Fig. 2-1

Use a sanding pad to sand away any rough spots left from the sprues or flash on the edges.

Fig. 2-2

they will be attached to the plastic frame they are molded on— this is called the "sprue." Sometimes parts may break off inside the box.

Look at the instructions. Take an inventory of the parts and get acquainted with how they go together. Look at each step in the instructions and mentally build the model first. As you gain experience, building models will become easier, but pay no attention to those who say real modelers don't need instructions. You'll avoid a lot of assembly problems if you study first.

Sometimes parts are positioned inside other parts. If you rush ahead, you may have to disassemble the model to install the parts you missed.

OK, now that you've read the instructions and checked the parts, it's time to get going.

Ready?

Fig. 2-3

If the pilot in your Stealth fighter has seam lines on his legs, shave the lines away.

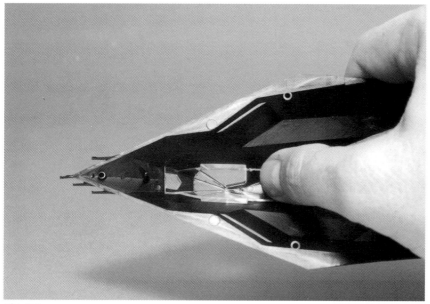

Fig. 2-4

First part in is the canopy. It just snaps into place.

Using nippers, cut the parts you'll need for the first step of the instructions from the sprue (fig. 2-1). Place the flat edge of the nippers against the part and squeeze. The parts should separate cleanly from the sprue.

There may be little rough spots where the sprues were attached. Use a coarse or medium sanding stick to sand away the roughness (fig. 2-2). Check for mold seam marks. These are fine raised lines on the edges of parts. Trim them away with a sharp blade or a sanding stick (fig. 2-3). In this case, the pilot had seam lines running down his arms and legs. It didn't take long to clean him up.

Unlike glue-together kits, you won't be able to dry-fit the parts—that is, practice fitting the pieces together. With snap kits, once you've pushed the parts together, they are nearly impossible to separate.

The first assembly is to install the clear canopy inside the top fuselage (that's aviation talk for the body of the plane) (fig. 2-4), and then place the pilot and cockpit inside before

All the parts on Monogram's SnapTite Stealth snap together easily.

Fig. 2-5

Before applying the stick-on markings, clean oils and finger-prints from the model with soapy water or Plastic Prep.

Fig. 2-6

buttoning up the plane. (The only paint called for in the instructions is to be applied to the pilot figure, but let's build this model without worrying about his appearance.)

Next, the bottom halves of the wings snap into the bottom of the fuselage. Then the top of the fuselage fits over the wing stubs (fig. 2-5), and the top halves of the wings go into the

remaining slots. The tail is next, then the stand.

Last, apply the markings. Before you do, wipe the model with a clean cloth soaked with soapy water, alcohol, or Polly S Plastic

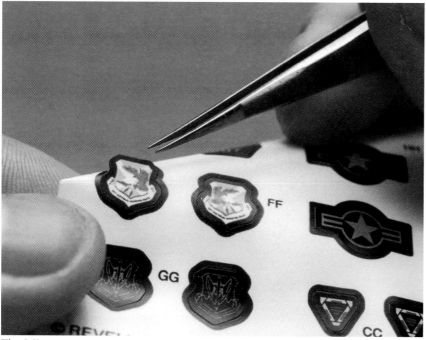

The paper stick-on markings peel off the backing sheet.

Fig. 2-7

Carefully position the stick-on markings with tweezers and press them into place.

Fig. 2-8

Prep (fig. 2-6). These will remove finger oils and mold-release agent from the plastic and allow the markings to stick better.

The last page of the instructions shows where the markings go. Locate each on the markings sheet, then carefully bend the sheet back until the corner of each marking lifts away from the backing (fig. 2-7). Pick up the marking with tweezers, position it on the model (fig. 2-8), and press down.

Place the model on the stand and admire your handiwork.

You've done it! Your first model, and it looks great!

3

A Hellcat out of the Box

Although it's more than ten years old, Hasegawa's 1/72 scale F6F Hellcat has good detail, fits nearly perfectly, and makes an ideal subject for painting with a spray can.

In Chapter Two, you got a taste for building model airplanes. Now it's time to swallow a lot of information. You're going to build a glue-together kit, paint it with a spray enamel, apply water-slide decals, and try a few professional tricks to boot.

The subject this time is a kit from Japan—Hasegawa's F6F-5 Hellcat (kit no. 617), a U.S. Navy fighter from World War II. It's simple, as injection-molded kits go, but it has good exterior details and makes a handsome model when finished.

As you did with your first model in Chapter Two, study the instructions and parts before starting. After cutting the parts from the sprues, clean up the sprue attachment points and lightly sand the mating surfaces of each part with a medium sanding stick (fig. 3-1).

Inside First

Assemble the cockpit using liquid cement. Dip the brush

Fig. 3-1

A medium sanding stick is used to lightly rough up the mating surfaces of all glue joints.

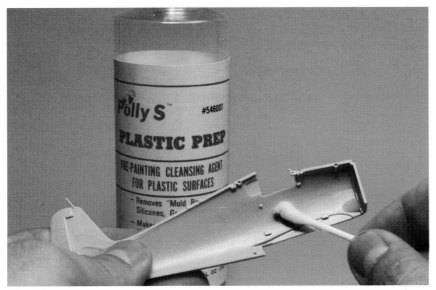

Fig. 3-2

Before paint goes on the model, remove oils and fingerprints with soapy water or Plastic Prep.

into the bottle and transfer the liquid cement to the model. Touch the brush to the seam where the parts meet, and the cement will drain into and along the seam. This will take a little practice, but you'll get the hang of it.

Liquid cement works and dries much faster than tube glue. If the glue runs onto the surface of the model (where you don't want it to go), don't try to wipe it off—that will only make it worse. It will evaporate quickly, but it may crinkle the plastic slightly. Paint will cover most of these blemishes, so don't panic.

The next step is to paint the cockpit and the inside of the fuselage halves. Use interior green for this cockpit.

But before you paint, wash the parts in soapy water or swab them with Plastic Prep (fig. 3-2). A clean, oil-free surface is especially important when using water-base paints. Oils will keep the paint from spreading smoothly and can ruin the paint's adhesion to the plastic.

Dip a soft, 1/4"-wide flat brush into the paint bottle so that half of the length of bristles is in the paint. Carefully stroke the paint on the surface of the model and make only two or three passes (fig. 3-3). Additional passes will only cause brush marks in the rapidly drying paint. If you need it, you can apply a second coat after the first has dried.

You can speed the drying of water-base paints with a warm hair dryer, but be careful not to overheat (and melt) the plastic kit parts.

Paint the Hellcat's cockpit with Polly Scale interior green using a flat brush.

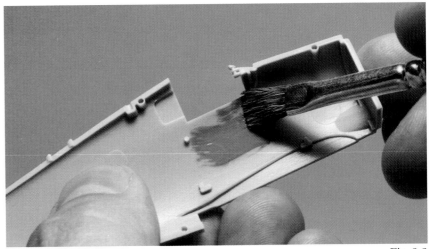

Fig. 3-3

Your first professional technique—seat belts cut from masking tape!

Fig. 3-4

Paint all the cockpit parts interior green. When the paint is dry, apply the instrument panel and console decals. We'll talk more about decals later, but for now, dip each item in water, let it sit for a minute on your work surface, then slide the decal into position with a brush or cotton swab. Let the decals dry for about an hour before touching them.

Buckle Up

Before you install the cockpit into the fuselage, let's try one of the professional tricks. Place a piece of masking tape on your work surface and, guided by a straightedge (a steel ruler), cut the tape into thin strips with a sharp blade. With a fine brush, paint little dabs of silver enamel on the ends of the strips to represent buckles. You have just created self-stick seat belts and a shoulder harness for the pilot! Pick them up with tweezers and drape them over the edges of the pilot's seat (fig. 3-4). Neat, huh?

Major Assemblies

Before you start gluing the main assemblies, test-fit the parts. This dry run will uncover fit problems and assembly wrinkles that you can solve before it's too late. Once everything checks out, you can start gluing parts.

Cement the cockpit into one side of the fuselage (fig. 3-5). Now you can cement the fuselage halves together. Touch the cement brush to a few points along the fuselage seam and allow the cement to flow along the seam (fig. 3-6). Now squeeze the parts together. The softened plastic may ooze out of the seam, but that's OK. Don't try to wipe it off or cut it away while it's soft.

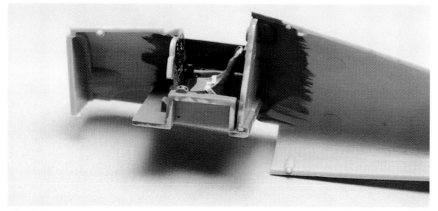

Fig. 3-5

Here's the completed cockpit installed in one fuselage half.

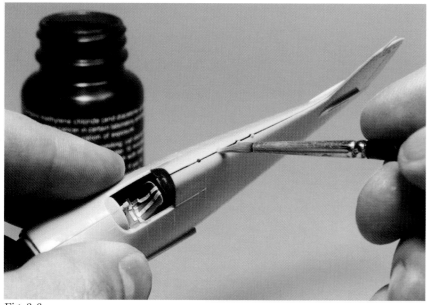

Fig. 3-6

Liquid cement flows along the seams by capillary attraction.

Keep your fingers away from the seams as the cement flows in. Sometimes the cement will flow around and under your fingertips and guess what? Yep, you'll have your fingerprints embedded into the surface of the model. If this happens, just let the cement dry. You can sand off the fingerprint later.

Build the rest of the model following the instructions. Be sure to follow the sequence so you don't leave parts out—such as the engine inside the cowl. Glue all parts with liquid cement, but leave off the canopy, propeller, and landing gear for now.

Make sure that the wing and tail surfaces are aligned properly. Hold the model at arm's length and look at it from every angle. You may find a part drooping a little. While the cemented plastic is still soft, adjust the fit so that the parts are in proper alignment as they dry.

Smooth Surfaces

Let the model dry for about an hour, then use a medium-grit sanding stick to sand away the oozed-out plastic along each seam (fig. 3-7). Inspect the model for rough spots.

Place a drop or two of gap-filling super glue into an old plastic bottle cap and using a toothpick, transfer tiny amounts to the areas you need to fill (fig. 3-8). The glue's syrupy consistency keeps it from running all over the model. Let the glue slowly fill the seam or divot.

Once you have the glue where you want it, you can set it immediately with super-glue

After the glued joints are dry, sand away the squeezed-out plastic with a sanding stick.

Fig. 3-7

Fill any gaps or divots with gap-filling super glue applied with a toothpick.

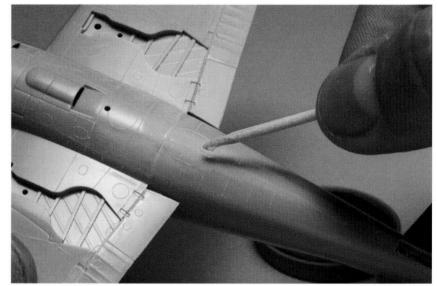

Fig. 3-8

accelerator applied with a Micro Brush (fig. 3-9).

Sand the seams with a medium-grit sanding stick and a few drops of water. The water keeps the sanding dust from clogging the grit. This is called "wet-sanding."

Wet-sand the filled gaps and inspect the model again. Sanding seams usually eliminates some of the recessed or raised surface detail. I use the curved no. 10 blade to restore panel lines by pressing and rocking it into the plastic. This creates a furrow that simulates both types of panel lines, and you have to look closely to see that it isn't molded into the plastic.

Preparing for Paint

Making a clear canopy look good is difficult. You can hand-brush the canopy frames (if you have a steady hand), but I prefer to mask the "glass" areas and paint the frames with the rest of the model.

Using a sharp knife, lightly cut a patch of Bare-Metal Foil, lift it from the backing sheet, and press it onto the area you want to mask. Use a cotton swab to burnish (rub down) the foil onto the canopy (fig. 3-10). As you burnish, you'll start to see the frame lines clearly impressed in the foil.

Lightly trace around all the frame lines with a brand new

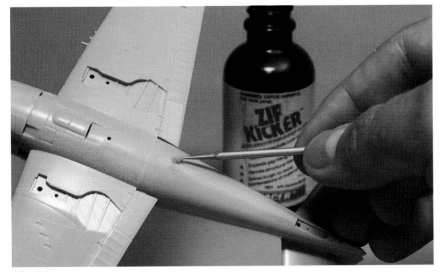
Fig. 3-9

Super glue (left) can set up instantly with a drop of accelerator. A Micro Brush is ideal for applying accelerator.

One of the best masking materials for canopies is Bare-Metal Foil. Burnish it down with a cotton swab (below, left).

After scoring along the canopy frame lines with a sharp knife, lift the foil from the frames.

Fig. 3-10

Fig. 3-11

no. 11 blade, then carefully lift the foil from the framing with tweezers (fig. 3-11). You may need to press the edges of the foil back down on the canopy window panes. Now all the windows are masked—the foil will keep paint from marring the canopy.

Attach the canopy to the fuselage with Elmer's black glue applied with a toothpick.

It's almost time to paint. Swab the entire model with Plastic Prep to remove oil and fingerprints (fig. 3-12).

Spray-Painting

The color scheme of this navy fighter was overall glossy sea blue, so you can paint the model using a spray can of Testor's Model Master enamel.

Since you haven't learned to use an airbrush yet (next chapter—no peeking!), using a spray can is better than trying to brush-paint the entire model.

The picture shows the Hell-cat model hanging by a wire in the spray booth (fig. 3-13). Shake the spray can until you hear the agitator ball rattling around inside. Make sure the nozzle is pointing away from you (duh!). Hold the can about a foot away from the model, but don't aim at the model just yet.

Aim the can just off the model, push the nozzle down to start the spray, then sweep the

Wash the entire model with soapy water or Plastic Prep before painting.

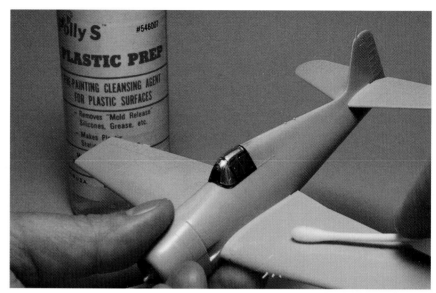

Fig. 3-12

Whenever you spray-paint, be sure to have adequate ventilation. This model is painted with a spray can in a spray booth with a powerful exhaust fan.

Fig. 3-13

spray across the model. Don't let up on the nozzle until you are aiming away from the model again. Paint droplets build up in the nozzle as you spray and spurt at the beginning and end of each stroke. You don't want to get a spotty paint job, so never start or end the stroke on the model.

Spray-paint the small parts while they are still on the sprue. You can retouch the sprue attachment points later.

Allow gloss enamels to dry for at least 48 hours before you handle the model. To remove the foil masks from the canopy, push the corner of each piece with a toothpick until it starts to pull away. Now grab the foil with tweezers and peel it off. If there is any foil adhesive left behind, remove it with a cotton swab moistened with rubbing alcohol.

Decaling

For some modelers, decaling is a nightmare, but it's my favorite part of any project.

The key to a flawless decal job is a smooth, glossy paint job underneath. Water-slide decals (provided in almost every airplane kit) are designed to stick to glossy paint. But many modelers paint with flat (matte) colors. What then? The answer is to apply a coat or two of clear gloss to the areas that will receive decals.

A decal on flat paint doesn't snuggle down tight, as it should. Air gets trapped underneath, and light bouncing though the

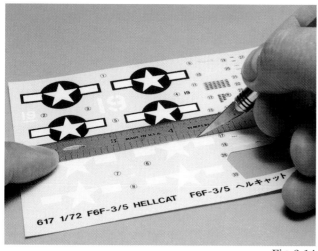

Fig. 3-14

Carefully trim excess clear film from each decal image by lightly scoring with a sharp blade. Don't cut all the way through the paper.

Fig. 3-15

Hold the decal in place with a brush while slipping the decal paper out from underneath.

decal's clear film creates a shiny, silvery look—a look you don't want on your model.

To keep silvering to a minimum, a glossy surface is a must. This model is already painted with glossy paint, so we don't have to apply a clear gloss.

I like to remove as much of the decal's clear film as I can. Do this by lightly scoring around the edges of each decal image with a sharp blade (fig. 3-14) before dipping the decal in water.

Study the marking placement guide in the instructions and locate each marking on the decal sheet. I like to work on one side of the model at a time. That way I'm less likely to damage wet decals while handling the model.

Cut each decal out of the sheet with scissors and dip it into clean water. Set the wet decal on your work surface and leave it alone for 30 seconds. Meanwhile, brush a little setting solution where the decal will go on the model.

Go back to the decal and grab the pieces of excess clear film with tweezers and lift them away and into the trash. Position the decal (still on the backing paper) on the model, then gently push it with a brush or cotton swab until it starts to slide off the paper. Pin the decal on the model with the brush and pull the paper away (fig. 3-15). Move the decal into final position, then touch the edge of the decal with a cotton swab to absorb excess water and setting solution.

You won't have to press the decal into position in most cases, but some decals that do not respond to setting solutions may need this persuasion.

Let the decals dry for 15 minutes or so, then brush on more setting solution (fig. 3-16). At this point, you do not want to touch the decals. The setting solution will soften the decal and sometimes makes it look wrinkly. Don't panic—just let

the solution do its thing. In another 20 minutes or so, the decal will suck itself down tight to the surface, even settling down into recessed lines and over raised details. It's a thing of beauty, but you must have faith. Just hide and watch.

Little Details

Snip the painted wheels, landing gear, gear doors, drop tank, propeller, and antennas from their sprues. Using a fine brush, paint the tires dark gray (fig. 3-17). Next paint the tips of the propeller blades yellow (fig. 3-18). When they are dry, paint the blades flat black, leaving the tips yellow (fig. 3-19).

With the model on its back, attach the landing gear and drop tank with super glue (fig. 3-20). Just a little drop applied in the holes with a toothpick will do it.

Flip the model upright and you're ready for another professional trick. You can make the

Fig. 3-16

An application of decal-setting solution will help the decal conform to surface detail.

Fig. 3-17

The wheel and tire were already painted blue, so a coat of dark gray on the tire makes it look like rubber.

radio antenna wire that stretches from the mast behind the canopy to the tail from stretched sprue.

From what? Remember, sprue is the plastic frame the parts come on. Roll a long, straight piece of sprue about an inch over a candle flame until it starts to melt (fig. 3-21). Be careful—don't let the plastic ignite. Remove the sprue from the flame and pull (fig. 3-22).

Depending on how fast you pull, you can produce long, thin rods of plastic or hair-thin strands.

For the antenna "wire," you'll want the stretched sprue pretty thin. Practice stretching sprue a few times to get the feel of it. Cut out a long piece of the stretched sprue for the antenna wires.

Apply a tiny drop of gap-filling super glue to the top of the little mast on the Hellcat's

tail and carefully rest the end of the stretched sprue on it. Dip a Micro Brush into super-glue accelerator and briefly touch the little mast. The super glue will set and hold the strand.

Now gently pull the strand taut to the main mast behind the canopy and repeat the gluing process (fig. 3-23). Trim the excess with the nippers or a sharp blade.

Fig. 3-18

Paint the propeller tips yellow and allow the paint to dry.

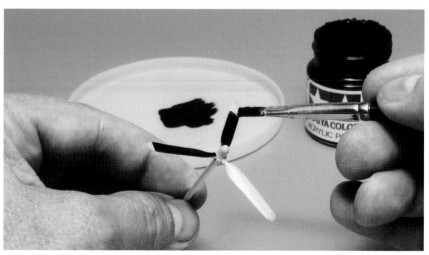

Fig. 3-19

Carefully paint the rest of the propeller blades flat black.

For added strength, attach the landing gear with a drop of super glue.

Fig. 3-20

Stretching sprue is easy! Hold a length of sprue over a candle flame, roll it between your fingers until the plastic is soft, and . . .

Fig. 3-21

. . . remove the sprue from the flame and pull! The faster you pull, the finer the strand of stretched sprue.

Fig. 3-22

Attach the stretched sprue to the antenna masts with a tiny drop of super glue. Don't use plastic cement, as it would melt the fine strand.

Fig. 3-23

The final touch is to color the wing-tip navigation lights. With a fine brush, paint the front corners of the wing tips silver (you can use either enamel or acrylic). When the silver paint is dry to the touch, overcoat it with Tamiya acrylic clear green on the right wing tip and clear red on the left.

Whew! You have learned a lot in this chapter, but this model looks even better than your first. I'll bet you can't wait for the next one!

4

Taming a Wildcat

Hasegawa's 1/72 scale FM-1 (F4F-4) Wildcat is a beauty and an ideal model for your first air-brushed paint job.

Here's another WWII U.S. Navy fighter from Hasegawa, the Grumman FM-1 (F4F-4) Wildcat (kit no. AP25). It's a fine kit, and you don't have to work hard to make it look great.

Still, we can find ways to improve the model and learn a few professional techniques for realistic painting and weathering.

"Weathering?" you may ask. No, you don't put the model outside and let the elements have their way. Weathering is the simulation of the effect of weather, wear, sun, and action on a combat machine. Weathering is usually accomplished after the model is painted, so the topic will come near the end of this chapter.

Improved Interior

We won't go over cutting the parts from the sprues and preparing them for assembly again. (Check Chapters Two and Three for a refresher course.) We are going to do something different this time, though. Let's add an aftermarket interior detail set made from polyurethane resin. The True Details

True Details resin cockpit and wheel-well castings are beautifully detailed.

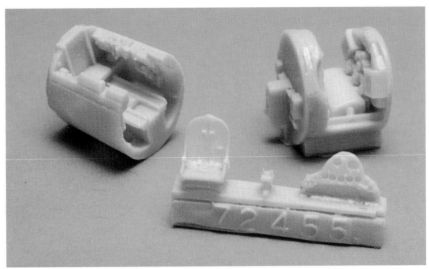

Fig. 4-1

Carefully cut the instrument panel from the "pour" with a razor saw.

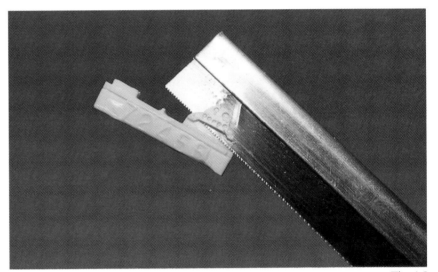

Fig. 4-2

set (no. 72455) includes a cockpit "tub," seat, instrument panel, landing gear bay, and a tiny gun sight (fig. 4-1).

Polyurethane resin is a relative newcomer to this hobby. It provides small manufacturers a way to create finely detailed castings without the expense of owning an injection-molding machine.

In its raw form, the resin is a two-part liquid. When the parts are mixed, a chemical reaction starts and the liquid turns solid in a few minutes. The castings are made in room-temperature-vulcanizing (RTV) silicone "rubber" molds that are formed from an original master carving.

Unfortunately, resin castings are impervious to plastic cements, and you'll have to attach them with either super glue or epoxy. I always use super glue and gap-filling super glue to join resin parts.

The True Details interior set is designed to fit right inside the Hasegawa Wildcat kit without modification. Since the kit has little interior detail, the castings greatly improve the look of the finished model.

These resin castings have to be carefully removed from the "pour," the resin stub that holds the parts (fig. 4-2). Use the razor saw and slowly separate the parts. A round needle file will clean the flash over the belly window opening in the cockpit casting (fig. 4-3). Swab the resin parts with Plastic Prep or soapy water and let them dry.

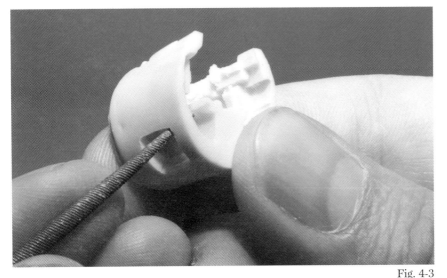

Remove the flash over the ventral window openings with a knife and round file.

Fig. 4-3

Behold the airbrush! With practice, you'll be able to produce beautifully painted models. This one is a Paasche H single-action, but there are several brands and types to choose from.

Fig. 4-4

Introducing the Airbrush

Perhaps the most important lesson you'll learn in this chapter is the use of the ultimate modeling tool: the airbrush.

An airbrush is a miniature spray gun, originally designed for fine art and photo-retouching (fig. 4-4). In this hobby, it is used to spray a fine mist of paint with precise control.

The airbrush, and its compressed air source, will probably be the most expensive tool you'll purchase in this hobby. But it's worth it.

Model paints should be thinned to properly spray from the airbrush. After thoroughly stirring the paint, I mix two parts of paint to every one part of thinner in a 35 mm film canister. I measure with eyedroppers. You can measure drops, or eyedroppers full, or bottles full—just use two of paint to one of thinner.

Use the thinner recommended by the paint manufac-turer. Mix the paint and thinner with a wood stick, an old paintbrush, or a piece of plastic sprue. Pour the thinned paint into the airbrush paint bottle or cup. Crank up the compressor or open the CO_2 tank valve and let's start spraying!

I won't show you here, but I recommend practicing with the airbrush on an old model. Read the manual that came with the airbrush, and experiment with the adjustable nozzle and spraying distances to discover how the

This time, airbrush the interior green inside the fuselage halves.

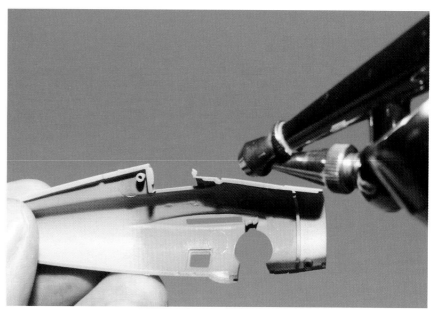

Fig. 4-5

Cleanliness is next to . . . clean leftover paint from the airbrush with lacquer thinner, cotton swabs, and pipe cleaners.

Fig. 4-6

tool works. You may have to adjust the paint-thinner ratio, the spraying distance, the air pressure, and the paint volume before you get satisfactory results. There's a lot to learn, so I recommend lots of practice.

Let's paint the cockpit interior (including the resin parts) first. Load the airbrush with thinned interior green paint. You want the tip of the airbrush to be about 2" or 3" from the surface of the model as you paint. As you did with the spray can in Chapter Three, start spraying off the model, sweep across, and release the air button off the model. You don't want a flood of paint, but you should be able to notice a buildup of color right away (fig. 4-5).

When properly applied, a flat paint should look wet on the surface for a few seconds. If you get a puddle that stays wet for a minute or two, you're applying too much paint. Reduce the paint volume by adjusting the nozzle, or you can back off an

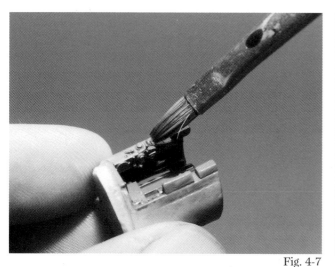

Fig. 4-7

A drop of thinned black paint accentuates the shadows in the detailed cockpit. This is called a "wash."

Fig. 4-8

After removing most of the yellow pigment on a rag, draw the brush gently over the raised details, highlighting them. This is called "drybrushing."

inch or two, or you can move the airbrush faster across the model.

Paint the insides of the Wildcat fuselage and the resin parts interior green. When you're done, toss out the remaining thinned paint—don't put it back in the paint bottle because the thinner will upset the paint's chemical balance and cause it to gum up eventually.

Put clean thinner in the airbrush and blow it through to remove most of the paint. Disassemble the airbrush and clean the parts with cotton swabs, pipe cleaners, and thinner (fig. 4-6). The airbrush's worst enemy is dried paint inside the nozzle or siphon. This eventually works its way loose and clogs the nozzle, or spurts out all over your model. Don't forget to turn off the compressor or shut the cylinder valve.

Wash and Drybrush

Time for a couple more professional tricks. To accent the cockpit detail molded into the resin castings, let's deepen the "shadows" by applying a wash. A wash is simply a little black or dark gray paint in a lot of thinner, flooded into the deep recesses of the parts.

Washes can be made with water-base paints, oil-base enamels, or artist's oils. The main concern is making sure that the thinner doesn't dissolve the underlying paint. A coat of clear, flat acrylic should help seal the base color before applying a wash.

Apply the wash with a brush and just touch it to the part (fig. 4-7). Let the dirty thinner flow into the recesses. When dry, the dark pigment remains, accenting the shadows.

The next step is to accent the highpoints by drybrushing. Use an old paintbrush for this. Choose a light color that complements the base paint. Since this cockpit is interior green, I chose yellow.

Dip the old brush into the stirred yellow paint, then rub the brush on a rag or paper towel. Keep rubbing until no more paint comes off the brush. Now you're ready to drybrush.

Lightly stroke the brush on all the raised details and edges (fig. 4-8). Not much will appear to happen at first, but as you stroke, leftover yellow pigment will rub off the hairs of the brush and lighten the highpoints.

The combination of darkened recesses and lightened highpoints will accent the molded-in detail (fig. 4-9).

Paint the instrument panel and control-stick handle black, then paint the molded-in seat belts light gray with silver buckles. Drybrush again, this time with silver to simulate wear on the seat and floor. Drybrush silver on the black-painted engine, too (fig. 4-10).

The finished cockpit looks great, doesn't it? Repeat the wash and drybrush steps for the wheel

Here's the finished cockpit interior with the wheel-well casting attached to the front.

Fig. 4-9

Drybrushing again, this time aluminum over the flat-black painted engine.

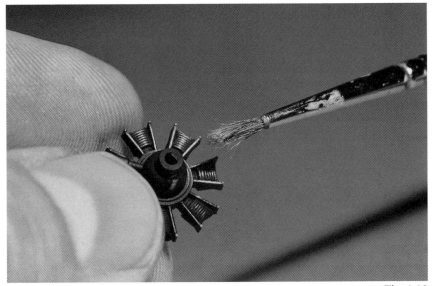

Fig. 4-10

well and install the detail set in the fuselage (fig. 4-11). Finish building the model according to the instructions, but leave off the landing gear, prop, canopy, and small parts.

Two-Tone Camouflage

This Wildcat features a gray-over-white Atlantic antisub-marine camouflage—a perfect training exercise for airbrushing. First, mask over the cockpit, engine, gear bay, and belly windows with masking tape—there isn't much overspray with an airbrush, but what little there is will find its way onto the areas where you don't want it.

Load thinned, flat white paint into the airbrush and paint the entire model. You'll need several coats to get com-plete coverage with white paint.

When the white paint is dry, load thinned, dark gull gray paint for the upper-surface camouflage. You won't need to mask the white, but you're going to carefully draw the division line along the fuselage with the airbrush.

First paint the top of the wing to get the paint flowing. Now spray onto a piece of card-

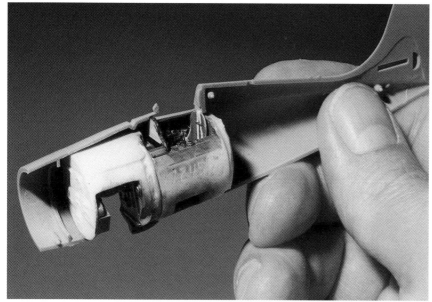

Fig. 4-11

The cockpit and wheel well fit perfectly into Hasegawa's fuselage.

Fig. 4-12

Preparing to airbrush, practice on a piece of sheet styrene. Here, spraying at an angle creates an ellipse with a sharper edge nearest the tip of the airbrush.

board or sheet styrene while you adjust the paint nozzle so that only a tiny bit of paint is coming out. You may have to move the tip of the airbrush as close as 1/4" away from the surface. Adjust until the paint flows out in a small-diameter pattern.

You can get a tighter spray pattern by tilting the surface of the model at a 45-degree angle from the airbrush. The spray pattern becomes an ellipse with a sharp edge nearest the airbrush (fig. 4-12). Maneuver the model as you spray so that the sharp edge of the elliptical spray pattern becomes the outside edge of the gray area.

Now move to the model and spray on the wing first, then move over to the fuselage while holding the air button down. Move the airbrush along the division line along the spine of the fuselage (fig. 4-13).

Establish the line first, then go back and fill in the rest of the gray areas. Depending on the colors you use, you may have to apply several coats. For best coverage, spray across an area for the first coat, up and down for the second, and so forth.

Airbrushing takes a lot of practice. Don't be discouraged if

After painting the entire model flat white, tune the airbrush to produce a fine spray of dark gull gray to form the color demarcation line.

Fig. 4-13

Use a fine-tip marker to accent the recessed panel and hinge lines.

Fig. 4-14

you don't get it right the first time. Or the second. Or the third . . . After all, I've been airbrushing for 30 years, and I'm still learning.

Here's a neat trick for you to add to your repertoire. After masking the clear canopy with Bare-Metal Foil (I painted it off the model this time), I sprayed the framing interior green. When it was dry, I oversprayed with dark gull gray. When you look into the finished model, you see canopy framing that is interior green inside, and dark gull gray outside!

Weathering

I wanted this little Wildcat to look a little used but not abused. After applying the decals, I oversprayed the model with Polly Scale clear flat to produce an overall flat sheen. When the overcoat was dry, I accented the fine recessed panel lines with "Gundam" markers (Gundam is a Japanese animated robot television series). These are fine-tipped black, brown, and dark gray markers designed for this purpose.

I used brown on the hinge lines and dark gray on all the panel lines. Simply trace over the kit's detail (fig. 4-14), wait for the ink to dry, then remove the excess ink with an eraser (fig. 4-15). I used a Pink Pearl, but it was too soft and took a lot of work to rub off the excess. A pencil eraser has more grit and works better.

Fig. 4-15

Remove excess marker ink with an eraser.

Fig. 4-16

Apply exhaust stains and gun-powder-flash stains using pastel-chalk dust and a closely cropped brush.

Use artist's pastel chalks to produce exhaust and gunsmoke stains. Rub black, brown, and gray chalks onto paper until little piles of pastel dust appear. Grab an old paintbrush and cut off all but 1/16" of the bristles. Rub the brush into the pastel dust and scrub it onto the model (fig. 4-16). Create stains that go backward from the exhaust pipes and machine-gun barrels to represent the natural action of the airstream. Feather the stains with a cotton swab. Work slowly; you can always add more. If you botch it, you can get most of the pastel chalk off the model with soapy water.

Your Atlantic Wildcat is done. More important, you've finished your first airbrushed model. Keep practicing with the airbrush at every opportunity. The more you use it, the better your results.

Except for a few small details that were hand-brushed, all the rest of the models in this book were painted with the airbrush. After you get the hang of it, you'll wonder how you ever did without it.

5

Rigging a Classic

Perhaps one of the most elegant combat biplanes ever produced, Curtiss' F11C-2 Goshawk is the subject of the old, yet excellent, 1/72 scale Monogram kit.

Monogram's little Curtiss F11C-2 Goshawk (kit no. PA210) may be 30 years old, but it is still a beauty (as are its companion kits, the Curtiss P-6E and the Boeing F4B-4). The parts are generally well detailed, and the fit is superb.

But the kit's age shows in two areas: interior detail and decals. These are easy to fix.

The biggest hurdle with any biplane kit is the rigging—the wire braces that kept early aircraft from coming apart in midair. We'll go through a simple technique to add rigging,

and we'll replace the kit decals with aftermarket items.

Quick Fix

The kit's interior consists of a pilot figure sitting on a pole that attaches to one side of the fuselage. No seat or stick is

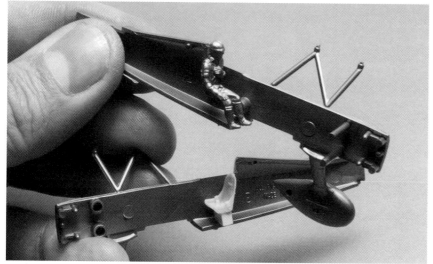

Fig. 5-1

The pilot figure, seemingly unsupported, looks dated. The addition of a True Details resin seat (with belts molded in) looks a lot better.

Fig. 5-2

Filling a molding depression is easy with gap-filling super glue applied with a toothpick.

provided, but a decal is supplied for the instrument panel. If you want the pilot inside, you won't need a seat—he'll take up most of the cockpit opening and block the view. I left him out and replaced him with a True Details resin seat (set no. 72411) perched on a couple of blocks of sheet styrene (fig. 5-1).

Occasionally, you'll find little round depressions in plastic kit parts. These are caused by the ejector pins that push the plastic parts out of the injection-molding machine. They don't look good on a finished model, so add a drop of gap-filling super glue and let it fill the depression (fig. 5-2). Touch a Micro Brush loaded with super-glue accelerator next to the glue and watch the glue set. Then sand the glue level with the surrounding plastic.

You'll find many kits with simulated fabric detail. Early aircraft had metal and wood internal structure, but the aerodynamic skin was often strong linen. When painted, the fabric is just as smooth as painted metal. Don't worry if you loose some of that texture on the model—it should be smooth anyway.

Glue the fuselage together and add the bottom wing. Don't put on the top wing or interplane struts just yet—we're going to go drilling.

Study your references to determine how the airplane was

Use a fine drill bit held in a pin vise to produce mounting holes for the rigging.

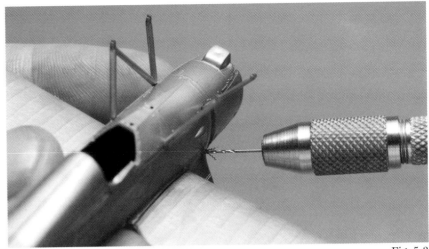

Fig. 5-3

With the rigging cemented in the holes in the fuselage and lower wing, the Goshawk looks like a spaghetti factory.

Fig. 5-4

rigged. Most biplane rigging braced the top wing to the bottom wing and the fuselage. The wires usually went into the wing fabric right next to the ends of the struts. Often these wires were paired close together. Find the attachment points on the wings and fuselage. Mark them by gently pushing and rotating the tip of a sharp no. 11 blade into the plastic. These are starter holes.

Next chuck a no. 60 drill bit in a pin vise and carefully drill all the way through the fuselage rigging points (fig. 5-3). Drill the hole at roughly the same angle that the rigging travels. Repeat the process on the bottom and top wings. Drill all the way through the wings and don't worry about the holes showing—we'll fix them later.

Rigging Material

You can use stretched sprue, nylon fishing line, or fine stainless-steel wire for biplane rigging. I used 6-pound-test nylon monofilament fishing line on the Curtiss.

Cut strands 3" or 4" long and place them into the holes in the fuselage. Place a tiny drop of gap-filling super glue in each hole with a toothpick, followed by accelerator. The glue anchors the strands in the fuselage. Repeat the process for the strands leading from the bottom wing. Now the model looks like it's growing spaghetti (fig. 5-4).

Position the top wing and interplane struts, but don't glue them in yet. Make sure that the cabane (over-fuselage) struts fit into the holes in the top wing,

Fig. 5-5

Rubber bands hold the top wing in place as the cement dries.

Fig. 5-6

Thread the fishing-line rigging through holes in the top wing and glue it in place. The next step is to trim off the extra line.

and that the interplane struts are in the holes in both wings. Wrap rubber bands around the wings to hold them in position (fig. 5-5). Add tiny drops of gap-filling super glue to all the strut attachment points and accelerate them.

Now comes the fun part. Thread a rigging strand through its hole in the top wing, gently pull it taut, glue, and accelerate. Repeat the process for the corresponding strand on the other side of the model (fig. 5-6). Work back and forth rather than

working one side of the model to prevent warping.

When all the glue points have set, trim the excess rigging with a sharp blade. Inspect each rigging hole and fill it with gap-filling super glue if necessary. Sand them smooth with the surrounding plastic and you're ready to paint the model.

Colorful Markings

Most of this aircraft was painted with aluminum-colored dope, so I used Testor's Metal-

izer nonbuffing aluminum. Paint the entire fuselage and wings, rigging and all.

Since I was going to replace the kit decals with aftermarket items, I also changed the paint scheme slightly—lemon yellow instead of white on the cowl ring and section-leader stripes on the fuselage and wing. I like the soft lemon yellow against the bright chrome yellow of the upper-wing surface.

I used Testor's Model Master enamels for the yellows and the red tail. I always apply a coat of

The painted model is ready for decals, gleaned from several aftermarket sheets.

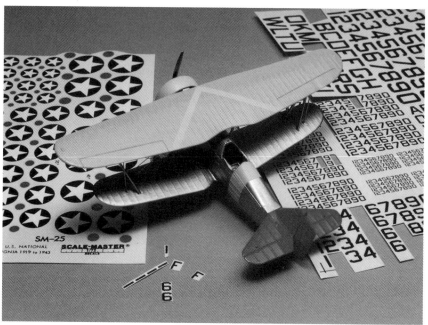

Fig. 5-7

Carefully move the tiny white numbers and letters into position with a knife.

Fig. 5-8

flat white first to keep yellows, reds, and light blues bright. After allowing the paint a few days to dry, I was ready for decaling.

I used the kit's Tophatters decals and the U.S. Navy legends under the tail, but I replaced the rest of the markings with items from Scale-Master and Super-Scale aftermarket decal sheets (fig. 5-7). I even applied the tiny letters and numbers on the tail one at a time; these came from a Microscale model railroad lettering decal sheet (fig. 5-8). Black stripe decals outline the yellow stripe on the wing.

That was easy, wasn't it? Sure, this was a simple one, but you now have the experience to take on more complex rigging jobs.

6

Building a Vacuum– Formed Kit

The tiny Temco TT-1 Pinto was not a success, but its dainty features and colorful trainer yellow paint scheme make it an attractive model.

Over the years, vacuum-formed kits have acquired a reputation as being models of last resort. But most vacuum-formed kits aren't really that difficult; they're just a bit different.

Vacuum-formed kits are manufactured by drawing a heated sheet of plastic over (or into) a mold. A vacuum-pump removes the air from between the plastic and the mold, hence the name "vacuum form." The molds for vacuum forming are simple and inexpensive compared with the tools for injection molding, so manufacturers often choose esoteric subjects. These include rare aircraft with limited sales potential and conversions for odd variants that manufacturers of injection-molded kits wouldn't find profitable. But limited runs mean higher unit costs, so vacuum-formed kits are often more

The Eagles Talon kit of the Pinto is an easy-to-build vacuum-formed kit.

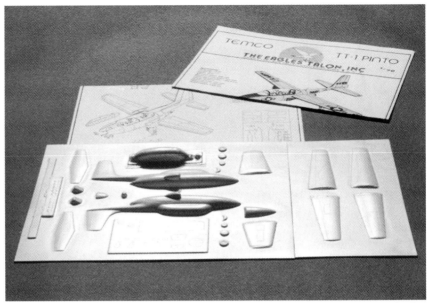

Fig. 6-1

The first step is to cut around each of the kit parts.

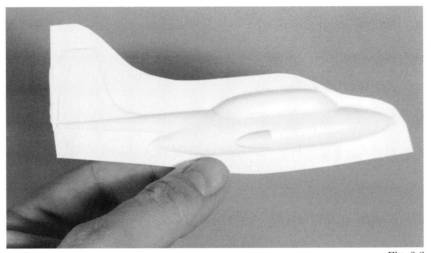

Fig. 6-2

expensive than injection-molded kits of similar subjects.

Some manufacturers cast delicate parts in resin or white metal, and some companies include decals. Most vacuum-formed kits come without these goodies, however, so we will learn how to use what we get, and look to other sources for what we need.

Start with something simple—really simple. If you choose a complicated model, you may be stumped, disappointed, or worst of all, put off from building another vacuum-formed kit.

For this chapter, I've chosen the little Eagles Talon Temco TT-1 Pinto (kit no. 114) (fig. 6-1).

Knowing the Score

The first two steps in building a vacuum-formed model are the most difficult: removing the parts from the surrounding plastic sheet and sanding the edges.

However, the remaining steps are almost identical to building an injection-molded kit.

Cut around each part, leaving a wide (and comfortable) margin of ¼" or so (fig. 6-2). Keep that excess plastic sheet; we'll use it for making reinforcement strips and bulkheads later.

With a sharp blade, slowly (and I mean slooowwlly) score around the edges of each part. Hold the blade at a 45-degree angle. Going slowly helps you

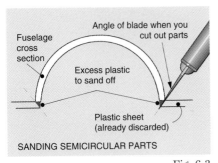

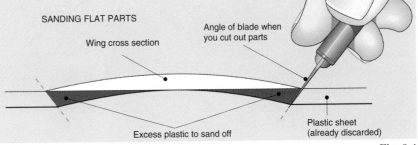

Fig. 6-3

Fig. 6-4

keep the blade from cutting into the part. Cutting at an angle reduces the amount of plastic you'll need to sand away at the edges of each part (figs. 6-3 and 6-4). Don't try to cut through the plastic with one pass; several light passes of the blade will do the trick (fig. 6-5). With the parts cut from the sheet, you're halfway to starting assembly.

You must remove extra plastic from each vacuum-formed part. The amount you are removing from the edges is equal to the original thickness of the styrene sheet from which the parts are formed.

Sanding the excess plastic is tedious, but it is the most critical operation. Therein lies the danger. Boredom breeds neglect, and you must pay attention during this phase.

Glue a 9" x 11" sheet of 240-grit wet-or-dry sandpaper to a sheet of heavy glass or some other flat surface. I attach it to the glass with spray adhesive. Place a cutout part of the kit and a few drops of water on the sandpaper and start sanding the edges of the part in a circular motion, checking your progress every 10 seconds (fig. 6-6). You don't want to sand away too much. It's a good idea to periodically change where you hold the part to ensure even sanding of the edges.

Hold On

It's not difficult to hold large parts such as fuselage halves, but there's not much to grab on a wing half. The drag caused by the sandpaper will cause your fingers to slip off the part.

Make a handle for hard-to-hold parts with a blob of sticky putty (such as Blue-tac or Silly Putty) (fig. 6-7) or with dou-bled-over tape (fig. 6-8). Make sure the handle doesn't stick out over the edge of the part.

Wetting the sandpaper keeps the sanding dust from clogging the grit and helps lubricate the sanding action. As you sand, the dust mixes with the water to create a slurry.

Fig. 6-5

After scoring around the edges of the part, snap away the excess plastic.

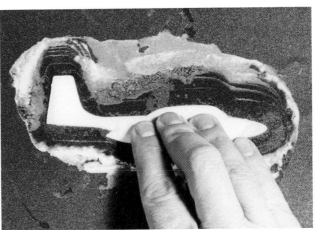

Fig. 6-6

The most critical stage of building vacuum-formed kits is sanding the edges of the parts.

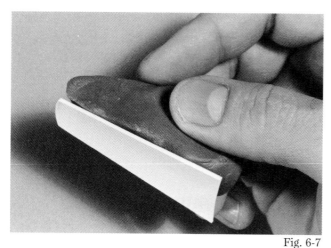
Fig. 6-7

Sticky putty makes an excellent handle for hard-to-hold parts like this wing half.

Fig. 6-8

You can also make a handle from a partially folded piece of masking tape.

Rinse the slurry from the sheet occasionally.

Many vacuum-formed kits have the vertical fin molded with the fuselage halves. While sanding the edges of the fuselage is routine, sanding the fin to scale thickness is difficult and time-consuming. So how do you sand the tail without going too far on the fuselage? Confining pressure to the fin helps, but the best way is to hold the fuselage off the edge of the sandpaper while you bear down on the fin (fig. 6-9).

Eventually, you want the trailing edge of each half of the flying surfaces to be as sharp as a blade (fig. 6-10). When the halves are cemented, the trailing edge will be acceptably thin.

After you've finished sanding the edges you can remove the opaque canopy form from each fuselage half and open jet intakes, exhausts, and vents. To open intakes, carve or drill a small hole in the center of the intake outline. Carefully enlarge the opening a little at a time with a sharp blade (fig. 6-11). Refine the opening with needle files.

The kit comes with a floor, seat pans and sides, and blank instrument panels. I found

Fig. 6-9

Hold the fuselage off the sandpaper while thinning the tail.

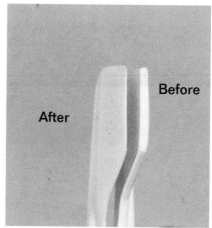
Fig. 6-10

This gives a good indication of how much material needs to be sanded from the tail.

Fig. 6-11

Open the jet intake and exhaust with a sharp knife and files.

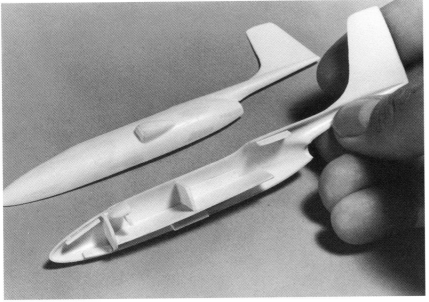

Fig. 6-12

Use sheet styrene for the cockpit floor, bulkheads, and the reinforcing strips along the fuselage edge.

better ejection seats in my spares box. As you install the interior, make sure the floor is placed low enough that the seats won't interfere with the canopy. Dry-fit the floor between the fuselage halves and sand the edges to adjust the fit.

Since this is your first vacuum-formed kit, don't worry about fancy wheel wells and eye-popping cockpit detail. As you become more comfortable with this type of kit, you can devote more time in these areas.

The Reinforcements Are Here

Solvent cements soften vacuum-formed kit plastic to the point of distortion, so I use gap-filling super glue on all assemblies. The thin plastic doesn't provide a lot of gluing surface, so cut six or eight rectangular tabs from the excess plastic sheet (I told you to save it) or styrene strip. Super glue the tabs inside one fuselage half so that half of each tab protrudes from the edge (fig. 6-12). These will provide extra gluing surface and reinforce the joints.

Place a drop of gap-filling super glue on each tab, put the

Gap-filling super glue holds the parts together and fills the seam on the fuselage.

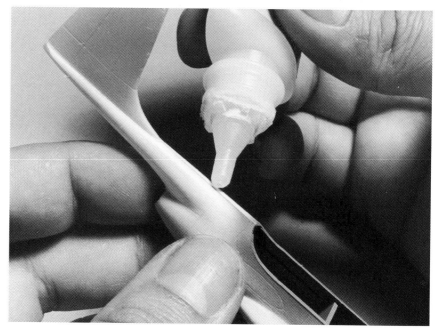

Fig. 6-13

Spread super glue between the vertical tail halves.

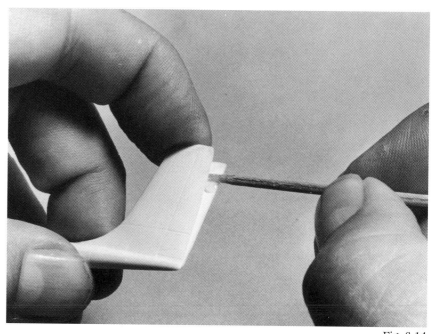

Fig. 6-14

fuselage halves together, and align the edges. Carefully apply a thin bead of super glue to the seam and allow it to flow into the seam by holding the halves slightly apart (fig. 6-13). Now press the halves together and apply accelerator. Sand the seams smooth with coarse, me-

dium, and fine sanding sticks.

Apply a drop of super glue to the inside of the fin surface, spread it with a toothpick (fig. 6-14), then squeeze the fin halves together. Wick away excess glue with a cotton swab.

Dry-fit the wing and stabilizer halves. Sometimes, I'll sand

flat the bottom surfaces of the top stabilizer halves and discard the bottom halves. That makes it easier to attain scale thickness.

If you find the wing halves aren't the same width or length, then align the leading edges and the tips and make up the short-fall at the trailing edges and wing

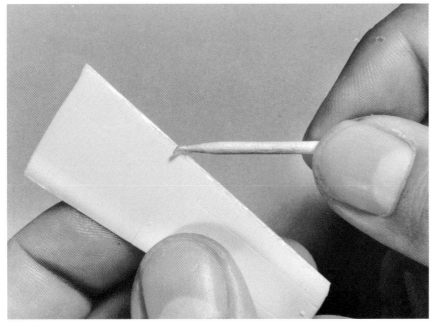

Super glue to the rescue (again) when correcting the shortfall at the trailing edge of the wing.

Fig. 6-15

Carefully super glue the wings to the fuselage. There are no tabs and slots to guide you.

Fig. 6-16

roots. I apply a bead of super glue along the step at the trailing edge (fig. 6-15), accelerate it, then sand it sharp and smooth.

The Pinto's wing positions are scribed into the fuselage, but alignment aids such as tabs and slots are absent. Since these wings are small and little stress will be put on them, tack them in position with two tiny drops of gap-filling super glue, checking to see that you have the proper dihedral (tilt up). To install the other wing make sure that it is placed at the same height, angle, and position on the fuselage as the first (fig. 6-16).

Once you have the wings aligned, apply gap-filling super glue to the wing-fuselage joints with a toothpick, accelerate the glue, then sand the joints smooth. Repeat this process for the horizontal stabilizers.

Now paint and finish the cockpit. Paint the walls medium

Repeatedly dry-fit the canopy to the fuselage and adjust with a sanding stick.

Fig. 6-17

A length of brass tubing makes a realistic exhaust pipe.

Fig. 6-18

gray and the instrument panels and seats flat black.

Carefully cut the clear canopy from its sheet and lightly sand the edges. Adjust the fit to the fuselage with a medium-grit sanding stick (fig. 6-17). When the fit is right, anchor the canopy with a couple of tiny drops of gap-filling super glue, then fill around the joint with black Elmer's glue and a wet brush. Water dilutes the glue and makes it flow into the joint. Wipe away excess glue with a damp cloth. Be sure the entire joint is sealed so paint doesn't leak in and ruin the inside of the canopy and cockpit.

Insert a section of brass tubing for the jet exhaust (fig. 6-18). Seal the inside end with sheet styrene so you can't see daylight coming through from the cockpit.

Most vacuum-formed kits include wheel halves molded in the plastic sheet, and some come with impressions of landing gear struts. I've never tried to use the struts provided (they have to be filled with wire and epoxy, and sanded to shape). Instead, I use

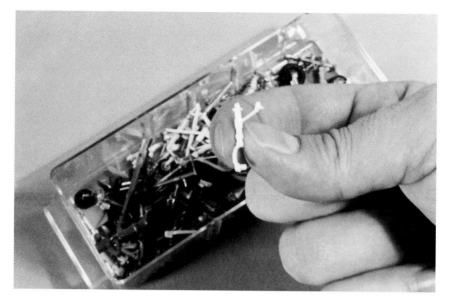

Fig. 6-19

Many vacuum-formed kits don't come with adequate landing gear, so fish through your spare parts. This set came from a 1/72 F-5 by Hasegawa.

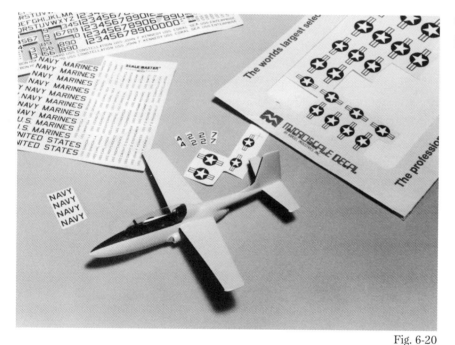

Fig. 6-20

Once again, aftermarket decals provide the markings.

them or drawings as guides to make new struts from stiff wire and plastic tubing. For my Pinto, I found suitable struts and wheels in my spares box (fig. 6-19).

Bright Yellow Paint Job

Mask the canopy with Bare-Metal Foil and airbrush the model overall with Testor's Model Master chrome yellow. Gloss enamels take a while to dry, so put the model aside for a few days.

When it is dry, mask for the flat black antiglare panel and deicer boots on the wing and tail leading edges. Use water-base flat black here; if you botch the black, you can easily remove it with soapy water without harming the yellow enamel. Remove the masks, unveil the canopy, and set the model aside to dry for a day.

No decals came with the Pinto kit, so it was back to my spare-decal collection. The insignias, letters, and numbers came from SuperScale and Scale-Master sheets (fig. 6-20),

With no pegs or holes to attach the gear, super glue and careful positioning supply the legs for the Pinto.

Fig. 6-21

but the intake warning stripes were robbed from a SuperScale sheet made for the Airfix Kaman SH-2 Seasprite helicopter. After a little cutting here and there, they fit perfectly.

Now all that is left is attaching the landing gear with gap-filling super glue (fig. 6-21). Make gear doors from .010" sheet styrene, paint them yellow, stick them on, and you're done!

See? Vacuum-formed kits aren't so bad, are they? Of course, this was an easy one, but the methods you've learned will allow you to take on a more complex kit next time.

7

Revolutionary Resin

This all-resin A-36A Apache kit comes from the Czech Republic. This one is every bit as good as a plastic kit but requires special techniques to assemble.

And now for something completely different: an entire kit made from resin! Well, OK, the canopy is vacuum-formed plastic, but the rest is resin.

Kits made from polyurethane resin are becoming more popular among enthusiasts. They look similar to injection-molded kits, but they don't require a lot of expensive machinery to produce. They are quickly becoming the darling of the "cottage industry"—the small, low-budget manufacturers who usually work out of their homes.

Some resin kits come complete with cast-metal parts, photoetched brass details, decals, and fancy packaging. But others, such as our A-36A Apache dive bomber (an early version of the famous P-51 Mustang) come with all-resin parts (yeah, I know, the canopy . . .), no decals, and no instructions.

This kit was made in the Czech Republic under the generic umbrella brand called Czech Masters. It was purchased from Aviation Usk in Usk, Washington, a mail-order dealer of unusual imported kits (Usk catalog no. 239).

Small parts are cast in a wafer of resin.

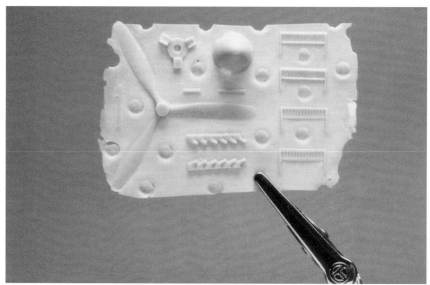

Fig. 7-1

Voids caused by air trapped in the resin when it sets are a common problem with resin kits.

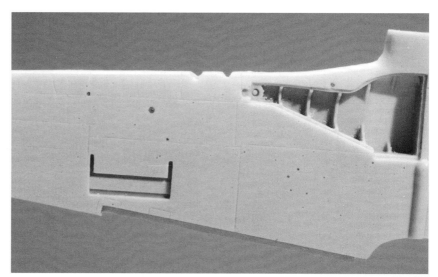

Fig. 7-2

Plenty of Detail

Early all-resin kits didn't have much interior detail, but this one has it in spades; in fact, there are more interior goodies in this kit than in many current injection-molded kits.

The problem is figuring out where it goes. Without instructions, you have to rely on reference material, experience with similar kits, and common sense.

Small parts are formed in two-part RTV "squash" molds—resin is squirted between the two halves of the mold, and the halves squeezed together. The resulting wafer of flash holds the parts (fig. 7-1).

Resin kits have some drawbacks. Air bubbles that formed in the mold-making and casting stages produce surface flaws (fig. 7-2). Voids are caused by air trapped in the mold as the resin sets. The little spheres hiding in the corners of some castings are caused by air trapped on the master when the RTV mold was formed.

Filling the voids is easy with gap-filling super glue (fig. 7-3). The spheres can be chipped away with a blade.

Heat can cause the thin castings to warp, as was the case with the A-36 fuselage halves (fig. 7-4). The easy fix is to apply heat once again and force the castings into alignment as they cool. Be careful, though, because the resin softens rapidly

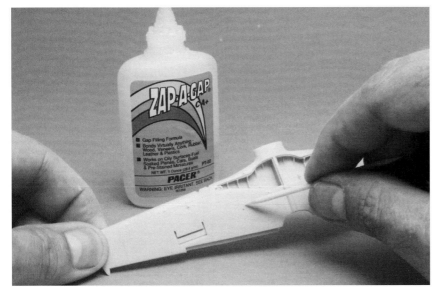

Fill the voids with super glue. A toothpick is an ideal dispenser of tiny amounts of glue.

Fig. 7-3

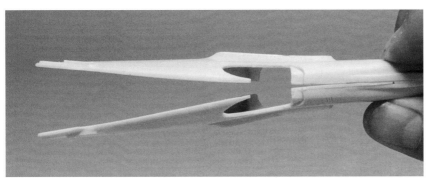

Whoa! What a warp! The easy fix to warped resin is careful application of heat.

Fig. 7-4

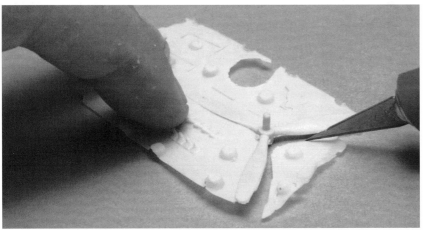

Carefully trim small parts from the wafer with a sharp knife.

Fig. 7-5

and you can easily make matters worse. Apply heat with a hair dryer, make small adjustments, then check the alignment. Repeat as needed.

Cleanup

Cut the small parts from the wafer with a sharp blade (fig. 7-5), and sand the edges with a medium-grit sanding stick (fig. 7-6). After cleaning all the small parts, sort through them and determine what goes where. I had trouble with the cockpit and borrowed a 1/48 scale (is nothing

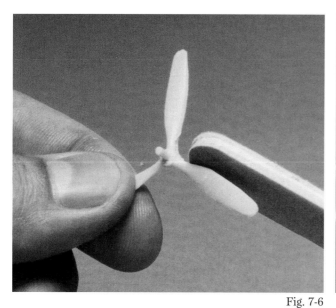

Fig. 7-6

Remove the mold-parting seams with a sanding stick.

Fig. 7-7

Assemble and install the detailed interior, along with the tail wheel, into one fuselage half.

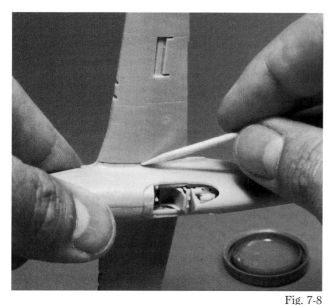

Fig. 7-8

Yet again, gap-filling super glue fills another seam.

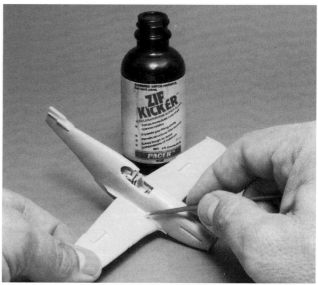

Fig. 7-9

And yet again, accelerator applied with a Micro-Brush sets the glue.

sacred?) Accurate Miniatures A-36 kit from a friend to help determine the configuration of equipment. One part that threw me turned out to be the mount for the tail wheel.

Use gap-filling super glue throughout, since plastic glues have no effect on resin. Test-fit the cockpit to one fuselage side and adjust the fit by sanding the edges of the floor and instrument panel (fig. 7-7).

Fortunately, modeling paints work on resin, but you must be doubly sure to remove oils from mold-release agents (if any) and fingerprints with soapy water or Plastic Prep. Paint the cockpit interior green, and detail as in Chapter Four, add the tail wheel, and close the fuselage (the photos show that I painted after assembly).

The one-piece wing features separate flaps and ailerons, which I added just before painting.

Fig. 7-10

The wing fit poorly to the bottom of the nose, but gap-filling super glue made short work of the gap.

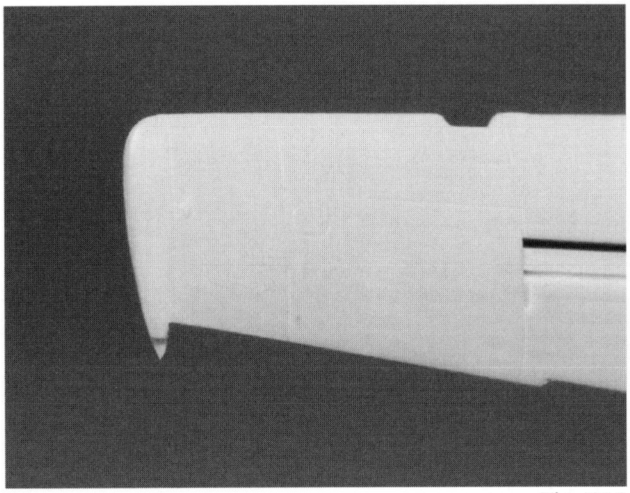

Fig. 7-11

Use super glue and careful sanding to reform the broken wing tip.

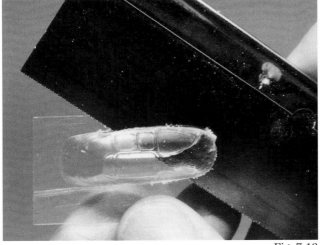

Fig. 7-12

Carefully cut the vacuum-formed canopy from its sheet with a razor saw. Refine the edges with sanding sticks and test-fit it to the fuselage.

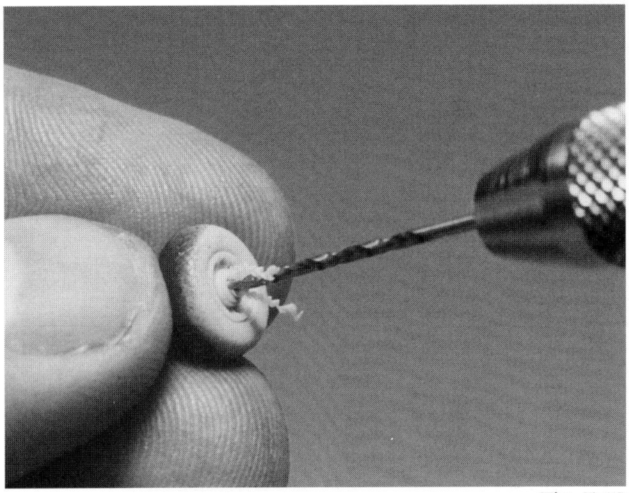

Fig. 7-13

Carefully drill out a hole in the wheel for the landing gear axle.

Super glue the wings to the fuselage (fig. 7-8) and check the dihedral. Accelerate the joints and sand if necessary (fig. 7-9).

My kit ended up a little askew underneath the nose, but I corrected with gap-filling super glue and sanded it smooth (fig. 7-10). The rear corner of one wing tip had broken off and disappeared, so I built it up with a few layers of gap-filling super glue (it must be in my veins) and accelerator, then sanded it to shape with a medium-grit sanding stick (fig. 7-11).

The vacuum-formed canopy must be removed from its sheet. I recommend using a razor saw for the rough cut (fig. 7-12), then refining the edges and adjusting the fit with coarse- and medium-grit sanding sticks. Install it with white (or black) glue and mask the clear windows with Bare-Metal Foil.

The kit's landing gear was finely molded, but the wheels needed holes drilled for the axles (fig. 7-13).

In keeping with the all-resin aspect of this kit (I know, I know, the canopy), I added True Details cast resin 500-pound bombs to the wing pylons. They only required a little work with

A little work with a fine file will clean out the fins on True Detail's 500-pound bombs.

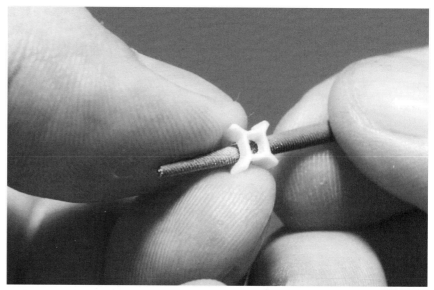

Fig. 7-14

Airbrush interior green onto the inside faces of the landing gear doors.

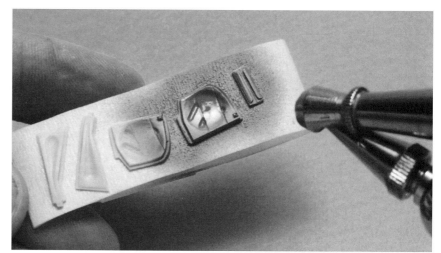

Fig. 7-15

the file to eliminate flash in the fins (fig. 7-14).

The kit's dive brakes were beautifully formed, but the flash partially filled the grillwork of the brakes. I fixed them easily by rubbing their backsides on 320-grit sandpaper until the flash wore away.

Mediterranean Service

Many A-36 dive bombers saw service in the Mediterranean Theater and featured the stan-dard olive-drab-over-neutral-gray camouflage of the period. Since the Apaches and Mustangs were new at the time, yellow bands on the wings and red spin-ners were applied to let ground troops and allied fliers know that these were friendly aircraft. With-out these colorful recognition features, the early Mustangs looked, at a distance, much like the Messerschmitt Bf 109.

After painting the insides of the landing gear bay and doors interior green (fig. 7-15), I applied a coat of white over the center portion of the wing, then followed it with yellow; the white coat helps keep the yellow bright (fig. 7-16).

The yellow stripes were masked and the camouflage ap-plied. I used Floquil Classic Military Colors on this model.

Since no decals were in-cluded in the kit, I found yellow serial numbers on an Aero-Master sheet, yellow-surround insignias from a SuperScale sheet (fig. 7-17), and letters for

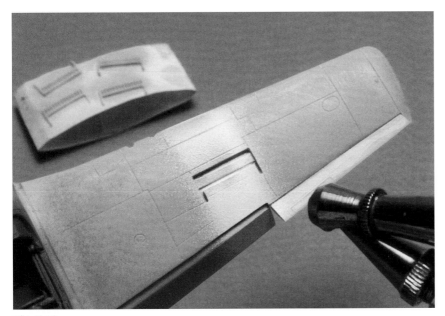

Fig. 7-16

A coat of white underneath will keep the yellow wing bands bright.

Fig. 7-17

What would we do without aftermarket decal sheets?

the nose on a Microscale railroad letters sheet. These were applied carefully, following a picture in a book (fig. 7-18).

Final touches included coloring the wing-tip navigation lights and attaching a monofilament antenna wire. Creating the landing light was a challenge; only a notch in the leading edge of the left wing is provided. I placed a pair of MV lenses (made for model railroads) into the notch with white glue, then wrapped a small piece of cellophane tape over the leading edge for the landing-light cover. I trimmed the tape at the adjacent panel lines, then hand-brushed camouflage paints up to the notch (fig. 7-19).

Now you can see the attraction of resin kits. They offer subjects not available in injection-molded kits, better-than-average detail, and a challenge to your modeling skills.

Anybody know what "Little Sie Michigan" means? Beats me. A model railroad decal sheet supplies the tiny letters.

Fig. 7-18

Also from the model railroad department of the hobby shop; MV lenses are perfect for the double landing lights in the leading edge of the wing. Note the deployed dive brakes.

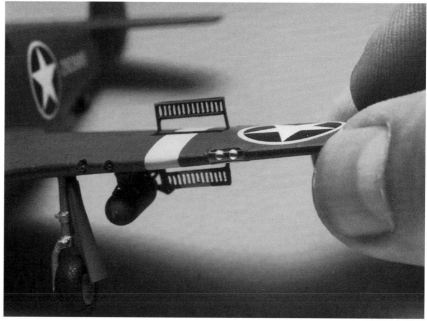

Fig. 7-19

8

Converting a "Hun"

The North American F-100C Super Sabre at its gaudiest best. Modifications to the plastic parts and the decals make this candy-striped Hun unique.

So far, we have been building model airplanes pretty much "out of the box"—using what comes from the manufacturer and accepting the version of the airplane as given.

Now, we're going to make a change. Let's take Ertl/Esci's fine North American F-100D Super Sabre (kit no. 8557) and backdate it to the F-100C version. This involves some "plastic surgery" to change the outline of the vertical stabilizer and the wings, and a few improvements to the kit. We'll also apply a realistic natural-metal finish with paint, and work up a really wild color scheme.

The subject is Col. George Laven's personal aircraft while he was commander of the 479th Tactical Fighter Wing in the late 1950s. He had it painted with bright stripes representing the colors of each squadron in the wing.

The First Cut

Let's start with the modifications to the vertical stabilizer. The F-100D (as given in the kit) had an enlarged vertical stabilizer (fin). To convert it back to the smaller C version, you need to reduce its height and width. To make it easier to make the

First, separate the fin from the fuselage by scoring along the joint with a sharp knife.

Fig. 8-1

With a razor saw, remove ⅛" from just below the trailing edge fairing.

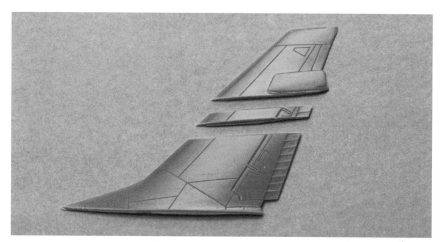

Fig. 8-2

modifications, remove the vertical stabilizer from the fuselage halves. Since this cut is on a slightly curved line, make repeated passes with a sharp blade until the fin breaks away (fig. 8-1).

Glue the fin halves together and let the assembly dry. Using a razor saw, cut straight across the fin in line with the top edge of the fluted rudder (fig. 8-2). Put the top of the fin aside for now. Remove ⅛" from the top of the bottom portion of the fin with the razor saw.

File away all but the bottom of the rectangular fairing on the top portion of the fin. What's left represents the fuel-dump fairing.

Glue the top to the bottom, aligning the trailing edge. You'll notice that the leading edge won't match up (fig. 8-3). Cut away the leading edge of the bottom portion. Fill the seam with gap-filling super glue and sand the assembly smooth, concentrating on straightening and sharpening the leading edge (fig. 8-4). The hardest part of this conversion is done!

Wing Modifications

All F-100s had automatic leading-edge slats. When the aircraft was at rest or at low airspeeds, the slats rolled down track arms to the deployed posi-

tion. As the aircraft accelerated, the airstream gradually pushed the slats back up to the retracted position. Esci molded the slats in the retracted position, so if you want to accurately model the aircraft as it would look on the ground, you need to deploy the slats.

Using a scriber or sharp knife, repeatedly score the leading-edge slat lines on each wing until it can be pulled off (fig. 8-5). Note that the top-surface part is wider than the bottom. Clean up the cut edges on the slats and glue the tops and bottoms together.

Sand the cut edges of the wing surfaces, too, then glue the

Fig. 8-3
Reattach the top of the fin to the bottom.

Fig. 8-4
Sand away the bottom of the leading edge so it aligns with the top, then sand the newly contoured fin smooth.

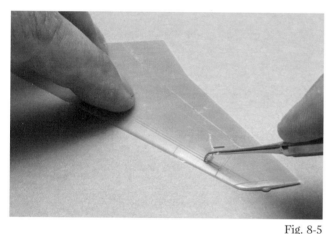
Fig. 8-5
Use a scribing tool to separate the leading-edge slats from the wing.

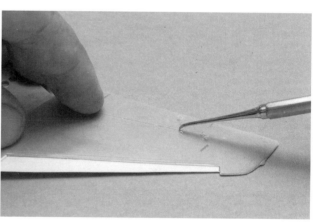
Fig. 8-6
The scribing tool cuts the new aileron hinge lines.

top wing parts to the bottom. Now you have this gaping hole at the leading edge of each wing. Cover the openings with styrene strip. You'll install the deployed slats after painting.

No Flaps

The other change made on the D model was the addition of landing flaps to the wing. This changed the layout of the ailerons and produced a kink in the trailing edge of the wing. To make the C version, you'll need to remove that kink, fill the recessed aileron and flap hinge lines, and scribe new aileron hinge lines.

Let's cut away the kink first, producing a straight trailing edge. Then file and sand the edge smooth.

Locate the aileron and flap hinge lines on the top and bottom surfaces. Fill all these lines with gap-filling super glue, accelerate, and sand them smooth. With a scribing tool guided by a straightedge, scribe new aileron hinge lines into the surfaces (fig. 8-6). In fig. 8-7, the wing on the right shows the kit's F-100D configuration, while the left shows the new setup with the straight trailing edge of the C model. I've used black ink to highlight the hinge lines. The new hinge lines should be the same on top and bottom surfaces.

Open That Sucker

One of the drawbacks of the Esci kit is the walled-off intake in the nose. To make it look more realistic, remove the wall

On the right is the unmodified F-100D wing. The F-100C wing on the left has the straight trailing edge and newly scribed ailerons.

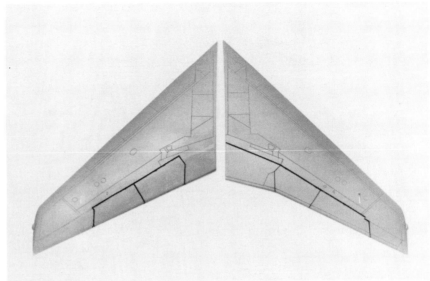

Fig. 8-7

After cutting the intake open, file the rough edges smooth.

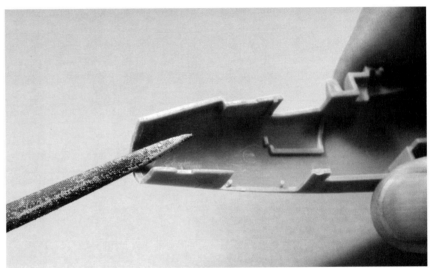

Fig. 8-8

A simple piece of sheet styrene serves as an intake trunk and fits underneath the cockpit tub.

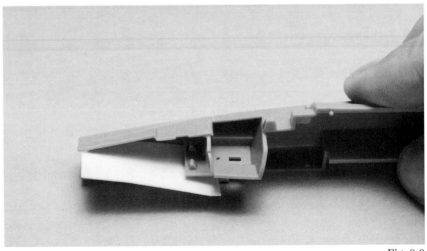

Fig. 8-9

Fig. 8-10

With the leading edge slats separated and sheet styrene covering the openings in the wing, the F-100C is almost ready to paint.

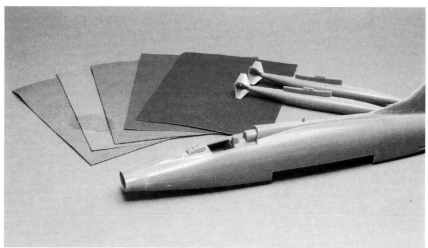

Fig. 8-11

A set of ultrafine sanding pads will polish the plastic as smooth as glass—important for a realistic natural-metal finish.

from the front end of each fuselage half with knife and file (fig. 8-8). Create a sheet styrene intake duct that tucks underneath the kit cockpit (fig. 8-9). The front end of the styrene should be flush with the end of the fuselage. Dry-fit the other fuselage half and adjust the edges of the sheet until it fits inside.

Close the fuselage and attach the intake lip and the severed vertical stabilizer. Dry-fit the wing assembly (fig. 8-10).

The wing fits so snugly without gaps that I left it off through the painting and decaling process. This made applying and polishing the natural-metal finish and complex decals a lot easier.

Shine On

After sanding all the seams smooth, I prepared to polish the plastic. Why? Because any natural-metal finish, whether it is silver paint, buffable metallics, or

foil, seems to put a spotlight on every tiny imperfection. Even scratches left by fine sandpaper will show through.

I used a Millennium 2000 polishing system (fig. 8-11). It includes a series of ultrafine sanding pads from 1,500-grit to 8,000-grit. Used in succession, the next finer grit polishes the scratches from the previous pad (fig. 8-12). When you're through, the surface of the plastic is blemish-free and smooth as glass.

Use each sanding pad in succession for best results.

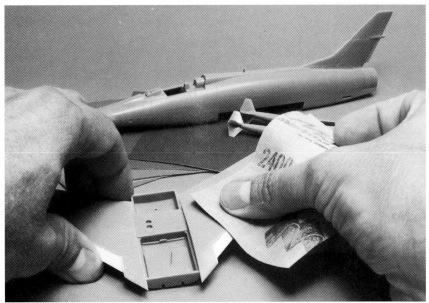

Fig. 8-12

A soft polishing cloth wheel turning slowly in a motor tool makes short work of polishing the SnJ Spray Metal finish.

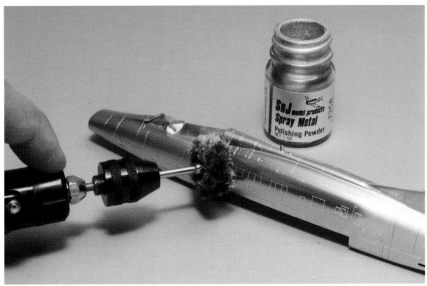

Fig. 8-13

Since this particular Hun was a spit-polished commander's bird, I wanted a top-notch metal finish. I combined two buffable metallic paint systems: SnJ Spray Metal (with its aluminum powder polish) and Testor's Metalizer (for the dissimilar panels on the wings and tail). These paints must be airbrushed.

I started with an overall application of SnJ. Several light coats were built up in order to avoid puddling. The result is a nice, but not spectacular, overall aluminum finish.

The next step really makes it shine. SnJ's polishing powder is worked into the painted model. You could apply it with a cotton swab and polish it with a cloth, but I speed things up with a soft polishing wheel on the motor tool (fig. 8-14). Just

look how shiny the center portion of the fuselage is compared with the ends. Be careful not to rub too hard or use too high a speed on the motor tool or you'll rub through the paint. If you do, lightly sand the area and spray again.

I masked and sprayed the center sections of the wings and horizontal stabilizers with Testor's Metalizer nonbuffing

Fig. 8-14

Since they are not included in the decal sheet, create the candy-striped wing tips with strips of solid-color decal.

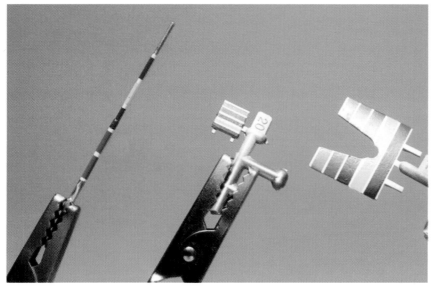

Fig. 8-15

Even the instrument boom (left), nose gear door, and speed brake got the candy-stripe treatment on Col. Laven's aircraft. Color these parts with decal strips.

aluminum to represent the dull, anodized surface of these structures. Then I sprayed Metalizer burned metal on the aft section of the fuselage. Metalizers are similar to SnJ, but are more fragile and don't utilize a polishing powder.

I lightly buffed the aft fuselage. This section was notoriously discolored by the hot end of the jet engine, and even a pristine commander's aircraft wasn't immune.

Candy Stripes

The 1950s were probably the most colorful years for the U.S. Air Force. There was no camouflage used then, and units took pride in dressing up their modern jets. Each squadron adopted a trim color and painted their fighters in it. Most of the time, squadrons were assigned to wings, under a wing commander who usually had his personal plane painted in colors representing all the squadrons of the wing.

Such is the case with this F-100C. Laven was known for having flashy paint jobs on his aircraft—he even had an F-104C Starfighter with multicolored stripes, an all-red tail with a

Fig. 8-16

huge Tactical Air Command badge on it, and whitewall tires!

But this F-100C just had to be the subject of my conversion. Creating the color scheme was complicated. I started with SuperScale sheet no. 72-357, but it provided only a portion of the candy stripes—the nose, fuselage, fin, and drop-tank stripes. Missing were the stripes on the wing tips, horizontal stabilizer tips, instrument boom, nose-gear door, and speed brake. The green and blue stripes on the decals were too dark, and the wing badge on the fin wasn't correct. I had a lot of work to do to get this model right.

I cut strips of solid white decal and laid them over the in-correct green and white stripes, then cut strips of bright green and blue decal to fit on the trim. All of this was done before cutting the SuperScale decals from the sheet. You can put one decal on top of another, as long as the bottom decal's paper doesn't get wet. The hard part was cutting the curved stripes for the nose and drop tanks. After several attempts, I had them right.

Next I masked the wing and tail tips and sprayed them semi-gloss white. When they were dry, I laid on colored decal stripes (fig. 8-14) top and bottom. (Low-tack tape covers much of the wings to protect them from fingerprints.) Some of the stripes continued on the separate leading-edge slats, too. I used the same stripes on the boom, nose-gear door, and speed brake (fig. 8-15).

The final touches were spraying the drop-tank fins in yellow, orange, red, and green enamels to match the decal stripes, and hand-painting over the incorrect wing badge on the tail.

All that was left was to attach all the small parts and snap on the wing. I decided not to create the leading-edge slat rails, since they would then be hard to see. But I represented the slots they sat in with short black decal stripes.

Put on your shades! Your first minor conversion is blinding everyone (fig. 8-16)!

9

Lights, Camouflage, Action!

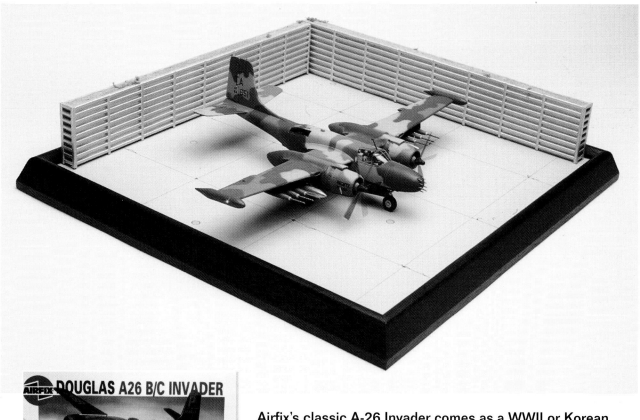

Airfix's classic A-26 Invader comes as a WWII or Korean bomber out of the box. Converting it to a Vietnam-era A-26K takes a lot of work. This model features working lights and turning propellers.

As you develop your modeling skills, you'll eventually want to push them to the limit. Of course, your limit may be higher or lower than mine, but I think I reached as far as I could with this next project.

It all started when I discovered an integrated circuit made for model railroaders by Richmond Controls (item no.

Tiny Miniatronics bulbs and the Richmond Controls integrated circuit are the keys to the Invader's light show.

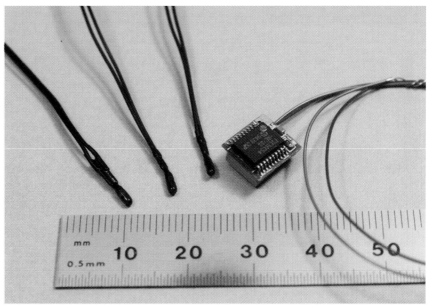

Fig. 9-1

More elements of the conversion (clockwise from top left): Paragon's A-26 resin flap set; Carpena decal; Paragon's A-26K resin conversion; and two small electric motors.

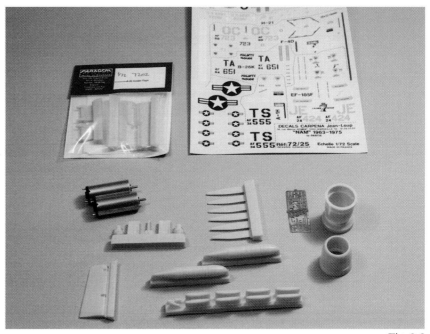

Fig. 9-2

941101-000). It is designed to fit into tiny N gauge locomotives and create realistic lighting effects (fig. 9-1). Depending on how you decide to wire it, the circuit regulates current for flashing, pulsing, or double-pulsing lights as well as steady lights. The circuit can run on a variety of power supplies, but the output can be used to light microbulbs or light-emitting diodes (LEDs).

At about the same time I discovered tiny Miniatronics "grain of rice" bulbs in red and green (1.5-volt, 30-milliamp, 1.2 mm–diameter) that would be the appropriate size for 1/72 scale aircraft models. I started to wire them together in my mind: "Hmm. A pulsing anticollision beacon and wing-tip navigation lights. Hmm."

Then I thought about a spinning propeller—that would be neat. A model in this small scale with working features might not be unique, but it would be interesting.

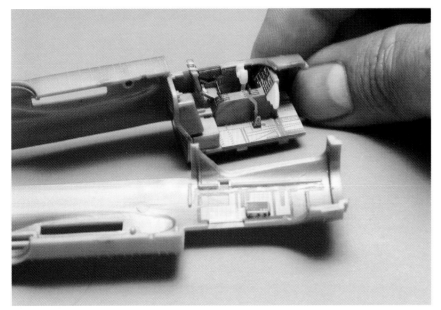

Fig. 9-3

An airwaves photoetched brass interior detail set improves the front office.

I started looking around for small electrical motors and found some inexpensive ones in the Edmund Scientific catalog (item no. A52-555). They cost only a few dollars each and were small enough to fit into some radial-engine cowls and nacelles. "Hmm. An airplane with working lights and a spinning propeller. Hmm. How about two spinning propellers?"

I looked through my collection and found only two candidates: A Hasegawa S2F Tracker, or an Airfix A-26 Invader. The anticollision beacon was applied to the Invader in Vietnam, and I had just purchased a Paragon resin conversion for that kit. . . . That's it!

Planning Ahead

This project took a lot of planning. I had to fit all the electrical components into the model, find a power supply, set up a scenario to justify the model's action pose, assemble paints and references, and then plan a course of action to incorporate it all into a good-looking model.

The first hurdle was power. The circuit needed at least 6 volts to work the lights. I found a couple of small camera batteries that would work—but they didn't work for long. After 5 or 6 minutes, the lights drained the battery. Too bad. I could have buried the battery in the bomb bay, and the model would have been free of connections to a base.

I resigned myself to using a Radio Shack transformer (no. 273-1454D), converting household 120-volt AC current to 6 volts DC. Now the lights work. How about the motors? Whoa! Six volts make those little can motors scream. That would spin the propellers to destruction. The answer was to install a variable resistor (Radio Shack no. 271-1605) to allow me to dial in the speed of the motors.

I had everything I needed (fig. 9-2): the Paragon resin A-26K conversion (no. 7201); a Paragon set of resin A-26 flaps (no. 7202); an Airwaves photoetched brass cockpit interior (no. 72-155); a Falcon vacuumformed canopy set (from Clear Vax set 10); an old out-of-print Carpena decal; Squadron/Signal's A-26 In Action book; the lights, motors, and circuitry; and the old Airfix A-26C kit (no. 05011). Eeew! Now there's a relic.

The huge, raised rivets and panel lines on the early 1970s-vintage kit had to go, so I sanded them smooth. Next, I installed the Airwaves interior. Most of the photoetched brass parts cover the kit floor, walls, and consoles and are an improvement (fig. 9-3).

I cut away the Airfix flaps and dry-fit the Paragon resin dropped flaps (fig. 9-4). I had to cut resin parts such as the enlarged rudder (fig. 9-5) from their pours with a razor saw.

To make room for the dropped flaps, remove the kit flaps. A sharp knife scores the separation line.

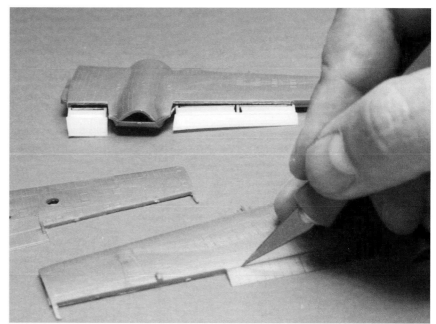

Fig. 9-4

Use a razor saw to separate the wide resin rudder from its pour stub.

Fig. 9-5

Routing the Electrical Components

I cut away the wing tips of the Airfix kit to make room for the resin tip tanks. The navigation lights had to be mounted in the tanks, so I drilled holes in them while holding them steady in a block of clay (fig. 9-6).

The wires pass through the wing and into holes drilled in the fuselage inside the wing mating surface (fig. 9-7). They are then soldered to the circuit inside the bomb bay.

The anticollision beacon high atop the vertical stabilizer is also connected to the circuit, so that it is on continuously but pulses brighter every second. The wires lead down the tail, into the fuselage and into the bomb bay.

All lights were super glued in place. When the wings and fuselage were assembled, I used gap-filling super glue to fair the bulbs to the surface. I had to be careful when sanding the super-glue filler that I didn't sand open the fragile bulbs.

Two Turnin'

Mounting the electric motors was more difficult. The cylindrical can motors were just

Fig. 9-6

Use a lump of modeling clay to hold the resin wing-tip tank steady as you drill a hole for the navigation light.

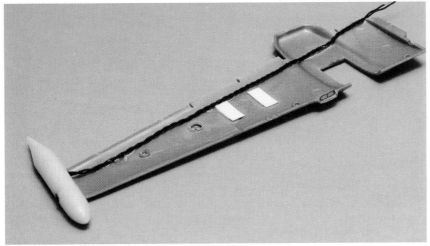

Fig. 9-7

Install the Miniatronics bulb in the tip-tank and lead the wires through the wing into the fuselage.

the right size to fit into the A-26 nacelles, just forward of the main landing gear bays. They had to fit through holes drilled in the forward end of the nacelle assemblies (fig. 9-8). I started with a small bit, then enlarged the holes with larger bits, then with knife and files.

The axles projecting from the motors were only 3/16" long. The props for this conversion are resin, so I had to connect them with the motors with stainless-

steel tubing (fig. 9-9). At first, I had inserted the next larger size tubing into the plastic kit engines to serve as bearing surface for the prop shafts. After I had installed the engines, cowls, motors, and nacelles, I found that the shaft would bind up and freeze. I ended up removing the larger tubing to allow the shafts a little more room. That solved the binding problem. The props don't spin as true as I would like, but at least they turn.

Since the props would be spinning at a moderate rate, I had to ensure that the blades were sturdily attached to the hubs. Brass wire super glued into holes in the hubs and blades did the trick (fig. 9-10).

Power to the Circuit

The wires to the motors also run through the wing and into the bomb bay, where they connect with the variable resistor

Drill a pilot hole through the fire wall of the engine nacelle. Enlarge it with knife and file to allow the mounting of the electric motor.

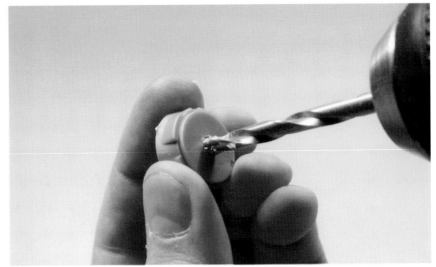

Fig. 9-8

Super glue the resin propeller hub to a section of stainless-steel tubing that serves as a prop shaft.

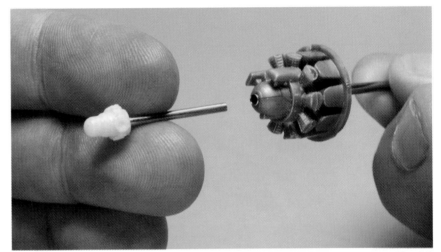

Fig. 9-9

Mount each resin blade to the hub with a short section of brass wire.

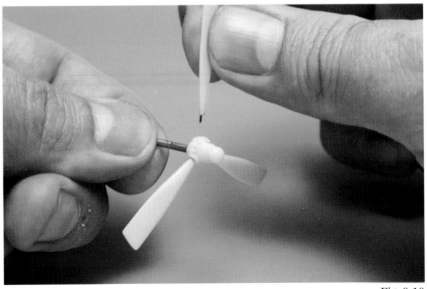

Fig. 9-10

Fig. 9-11

The variable resistor just fits behind the rear cockpit bulkhead.

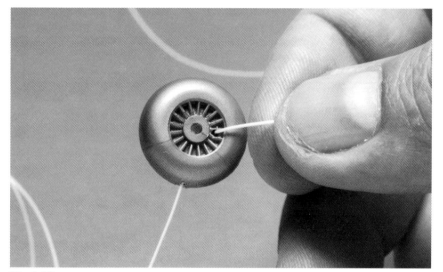
Fig. 9-12

Power leads are fine wire-wrapped wire coming up through the main-gear tires and masquerading as hydraulic brake lines.

that is mounted on the back side of the cockpit's rear bulkhead (fig. 9-11).

All these circuits were connected to the power leads. These are two strands of wire-wrap wire coming up through holes in the diorama base and into the main-gear tires (fig. 9-12). The wires masquerade as brake lines coming out of the wheel hubs, up the struts, and into the nacelles. They then run through the wings and into the bomb bay, where they split off to the resistor and the integrated circuit (fig. 9-13).

It's important to repeatedly test the circuit and motors as you put it all together. You don't want to get the entire model completed only to discover that something isn't working. The drawing shows the wiring diagram for all the electricals in the model (fig. 9-14).

Tight Camouflage

The rest of the project seemed simple compared with the electrical stage. I attached all the resin conversion pieces to the plastic kit parts with super glue. To fill the gaps at the trailing edges of the wing, I inserted styrene strips, then added the Paragon flaps.

Since the model was going to look as though it was about to taxi, I had to add crew figures to the cockpit. I found a couple of candidates, painted them, and parked them inside.

After fitting and masking

Fig. 9-13

Here's a view of the bottom of the model, revealing the jumble of wires in the bomb bay. The wires coming out of the tires will connect with the power supply underneath the diorama base.

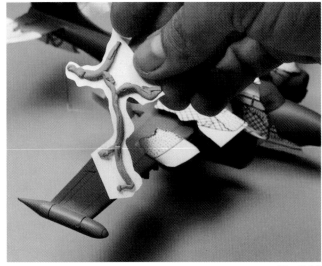

Fig. 9-15

Thin rolls of Blue-Tak putty hold the paper camouflage-pattern templates above the surface of the model. This "loose mask" technique produces almost-sharp color demarcation lines.

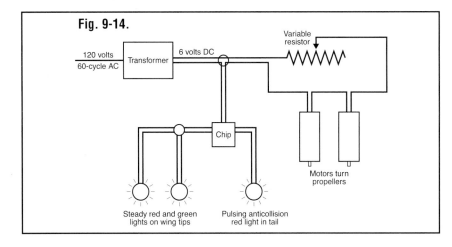

Fig. 9-14.

120 volts / 60-cycle AC — Transformer — 6 volts DC

Variable resistor

Chip

Motors turn propellers

Steady red and green lights on wing tips

Pulsing anticollision red light in tail

the Falcon vacuum-formed canopies, I was ready to paint. First I painted the model overall tan (Floquil FS 30219). I painted right over the lights, too. The bulbs shine right through the resin tip tanks, so the paint hides all but the very tips of the bulbs.

To produce the complex camouflage pattern, I first enlarged the official camouflage diagram to 1/72 scale. I then cut out the tan portions of the diagram, and placed them on the model with thin rolls of Blue-tac sticky putty (fig. 9-15). The putty holds the paper masks in place, but holds them slightly above the surface (fig. 9-16). When the next color is airbrushed, the raised masks produce a slightly soft edge to the color demarcations.

The next color was green (FS 34102), and I sprayed all the exposed surfaces. I repeated the masking stage, covering all the green areas with paper masks, then airbrushed the remaining exposed areas with dark green (FS 34079).

All the masks were removed, revealing the colorful topside camouflage. The bottom of the A-26K was black, so I soft-masked the edges and airbrushed Testor's Model Master flat black.

Next up was adding the decals. A little clear gloss was applied to keep the decals from silvering. There weren't many markings on these ships—not even national insignias—just tail codes and serials, and the Mighty Mouse legends on the cowls and propeller warning stripes on the nose.

After the decals had dried, I overcoated the entire model with clear flat, producing a nice, even surface. With a polishing stick, I carefully wore the paint

After painting the entire model tan, mask the tan areas of the camouflage scheme and the model is ready for the addition of the first green color.

Fig. 9-16

The diorama base consists of a painted piece of clear-acrylic sheet, a wood picture frame, and an out-of-production plaster revetment.

Fig. 9-17

from the three light bulbs and tested the circuits again. Great! Everything was working.

The Moment of Truth

It was time to attach the prop shafts to the electric motors. I dry-fitted them several times, making sure the shafts weren't too long and fit snugly on the motor axles. Just a tiny drop of super glue was inserted in the end of the prop shafts, and the props pushed home. If there was too much glue, it might squish onto the motor and gum it up. Too little glue would cause the props to come loose while running and go shooting across the room! I hooked up the power leads to the transformer to make sure everything was working. Yes!

The masks were removed from the canopies, and the paint job was touched up with a fine-tip brush.

Now I could attach 500-pound bombs with fuse extenders and napalm canisters (with their fins cut off) from Hasegawa's Weapons Set 1 (no. X72-1)

Draw concrete slab division lines on the base with a fine-tip marker.

Fig. 9-18

to the wing pylons. Last on the model was a forest of photoetched antennas (mostly on the belly). I carefully attached them with super glue and painted them to match the surrounding camouflage.

Basic Base

I needed a base to hide the wires leading to the electrical features. Since these Vietnam warbirds were frequently parked in revetments, I resurrected an old plaster set I had painted years ago to set the scene (fig. 9-17). These rest on a concrete-painted sheet of clear acrylic (Plexiglas). I used a fine-tipped marker to draw in the concrete slab division lines (fig. 9-18).

The power leads from the model fit into holes drilled in the acrylic base and are then wrapped to the exposed leads from the 6-volt transformer. The transformer is simply plugged into a wall outlet, and the model has power.

The variable resistor is touchy, but can keep the motor speeds at acceptable revs. I have to adjust it now and then, so I left off the bomb bay doors. When the model is parked in the revetment, viewers can't see the open belly, so that isn't a problem.

A couple of additions of ground equipment and personnel complete the scene.

10

On Display

Our cover subject, the 50th Anniversary tribute to the Blue Angels, is a ceiling-hanging display. One of each of the types the Angels flew in flight demonstration is represented in 1/72 scale. Acrylic rods covered with fuzzy white fabric "smoke" make the display possible.

What good is a well-built model if you can't show it off? OK, maybe you enjoyed the project, and it's always been your favorite airplane, but then what? I don't want to get existential here, but what is the purpose of a model?

Certainly, building models is a craft, and showing the model is an expression of pride. Entering and winning contests can satisfy our competitive nature. If you build models only to please yourself, fine. But why not please others while you're at it? Be proud of your efforts. Put them on display for all to see. With all the research modelers accomplish as they prepare their models, why not pass it on to others? Modeling is educational, so educate your audience.

Labels

A model by itself or with others only begs the question

Fig. 10-1
It's important to label models to inform your audience.

Fig. 10-2

A simple display base adds formality to any model.

Fig. 10-3

Prototype and production: A modified Monogram kit and a later Minicraft/Academy F-15C show the development of the Eagle's shape and color scheme.

Models make ideal presents. This Hasegawa F-106A Delta Dart was a going-away gift. The acrylic rod up the tailpipe was tinted with Tamiya clear orange to simulate afterburner flame.

Fig. 10-4

Feline siblings: Two Monogram F7F Tigercats show the development of the graceful twin-engined fighter. The "flying" F7F-3N night fighter is mounted on an acrylic rod.

Fig. 10-5

"So what?" You may not have a chance to explain what the model represents to your viewers. Instead, tell the story with a simple label (fig. 10-1). Tell as much or as little as you like, but keep in mind that the casual viewer probably won't want to spend more than 15 seconds reading a label. I make a label for each model I build. I simply type it on my computer, print it on fancy paper, spray-mount it to matte board, cut it to size, and park it next to my model.

An old Revell F-111A and a Hasegawa F-111F were issued 20 years apart, but they show the differences of the Aardvark's appearance through the decades.

Fig. 10-6

Story Lines

I tend to think of models in groups: family histories, stages of development, firsts and lasts, unit histories, a pilot's personal mounts, and so on.

Simple scenes or formal bases transform even a simple model into a "presentation." The Wildcat from Chapter Three looks even better on a simple plaque with an out-of-production Verlinden paper representation of a carrier deck (fig. 10-2). Take a look at this pair of Monogram F7F Tigercats (one converted to a night fighter) (fig. 10-5). One is posed on the tarmac while its companion flies overhead mounted on a bent acrylic rod.

Models can become gifts. This 1/72 Hasegawa F-106 Delta Dart in Montana Air Guard markings was given as a farewell gift to a person who was movin' to Montana (fig. 10-4). (This man went on to become a dental-floss tycoon.)

You can show the changes in shape and color of a plane as it went through its history. The F-15s (fig. 10-3) and F-111s (fig. 10-6) exhibit the colorful prototype markings and the camouflage later applied for combat.

The biggest theme display I've made is a mobile of the 50-year history of the Blue Angels. My idea was to show one of each of the different types of aircraft the Angels have flown. This display would not be a recreation of an actual event, since the different types never flew together, but it would be illustrative of what the Angels do as well as show the history.

Posing the different aircraft shapes in a diamond or delta formation would look awkward, so I studied the Blue Angel's flight routine for a likely pose. Near the end of the Angels' show, the team climbs to altitude and dives in tight formation. A few thousand feet off the ground the team splits off in dif-

ferent directions. That's it! Curving vapor trails from a single point in the sky (OK, from the ceiling of the room) would spotlight each model equally, look natural, and still show the history of the team.

Now, how could I do that? The models weren't the problem; most of them were readily available in hobby shops (fig. 10-7). The ancient Aurora F7U-1 Cutlass was bought from a collector and cleaned up considerably. The rest of the models were built out of the box (fig. 10-8) with landing gear retracted and pilots installed.

Painting involved a few different shades of blue with Bare-Metal Foil for the unpainted leading edges of the flying surfaces and intakes of the jets.

Decals were a problem, though. Some of the kits came with Blue Angel markings, but others needed aftermarket decals from SuperScale. I had two sets of decals for every model.

Fig. 10-7

The way you display models is just as important as how you build them. Think about story lines; the why's, the what's, the when's. This collection of 1/72 scale navy fighter kits becomes a 50th Anniversary tribute to the Navy's Blue Angels.

Most of the yellow markings were translucent and showed the blue paint underneath. A second set of decals, carefully laid over the first, produced bright yellow markings (figs. 10-9, 10-10, 10-11).

Mobile Mount

Posing aircraft models in flight presents problems. You need a sturdy mount but one that is unobtrusive. I like to use clear acrylic rod. It comes in several diameters and as long as 6 feet. I insert sections of brass tubing (fig. 10-12) into the jet pipes of the models to hold the ends of the acrylic rods (fig. 10-13).

A friend bent the rods by heating them and forming them over a curved plywood template. The other end of the rods for the Blue Angel display fit into holes drilled in a piece of plywood (fig. 10-14). The holes were drilled at an angle so that the

weight would bind the rods against the wood. A screw eye in the center of the plywood disc attaches the mobile to a ceiling swag hook.

Smoke On!

As unobtrusive as acrylic rod is, I wanted to cover it and make it look like the smoke trails of typical flight demonstration aircraft. (Smoke is created by injecting light oil

Fig. 9-8

Here are the Angels before they were Blue. Back row (left to right): Hasegawa F6F-5 Hellcat, Monogram F8F-2 Bearcat, Hasegawa F9F-2 (converted to a -5) Panther, Hasegawa F9F-8 Cougar, and a rare Aurora F7U-1 Cutlass. Front row: Hasegawa F11F-1 Tiger, Fujimi F-4J Phantom II, Fujimi A-4F Skyhawk, and a Hasegawa F/A-18A Hornet.

Fig. 10-9

Fig. 10-10

To make the translucent yellow makings show up well on the blue-painted models, I carefully over-laid a duplicate set after the first decals were dry.

Fig. 10-11

I super glued telescope sections of brass tubing inside the tail pipes of each jet.

Fig. 10-12

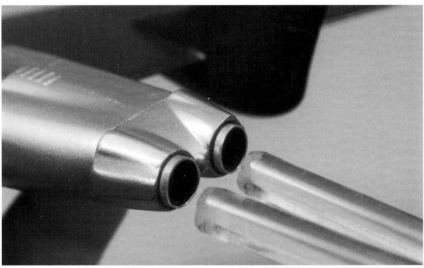

Acrylic rods fit inside the brass tubing of the Blue Angel Cutlass.

Fig. 10-13

Without its smoky camouflage, the plywood disc reveals the terminus of the acrylic rods and the screw eye that hangs from a ceiling swag hook.

Fig. 10-14

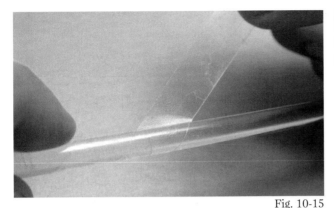

Fig. 10-15

Wrap double-sided Scotch tape around the acrylic rods.

Fig. 10-16

Wind a strip of fuzzy white fabric around the acrylic rod.

The finished Monogram Bearcat features a clear plastic disc to simulate the spinning propeller. Bare-Metal Foil highlights the leading edges of the wings and tail.

Fig. 10-17

into the hot engine exhaust—see, I told you that modeling is educational!)

Instead of burning oil, I settled on inexpensive, white fuzzy fabric attached to the rods with double-sided tape (fig. 10-15). I simply cut a one-inch-wide strip of fabric and wrapped it around the rod (fig. 10-16).

I simulated the spinning propellers for the Hellcat and the Bearcat by first chopping off the kit blades from the propeller hubs. I sanded the hubs smooth, then cut discs of clear plastic to size to simulate the arc of the propeller. I tried spraying flat black and gunmetal onto the discs to simulate the position of the blades, but that looked awful. I settled on light applications of clear flat. Then I masked all but the rim of the discs and airbrushed yellow for the blade tips—a light coat nearly all the way around, but heavy at the blade locations. The effect is pretty neat (fig. 10-17).

Even though the propeller-driven Hellcat and Bearcat weren't smoke-equipped, I mounted them to fabric-covered rods, too. The display would have looked inconsistent if I hadn't. The prop planes are mounted with brass wires embedded in the rods. These fit into small holes drilled in the ends of each fuselage.

The display is set up so that the airplanes are at average eye level when hung from the typical 8-foot ceiling. For higher ceilings, I attach picture-hanging wire to the plywood disc and cover it with a fabric-covered paper cone.

EPILOGUE

I have many, many, many more models to build for my collection of 1/72 scale U.S. military aircraft. One thing I've noticed over the years: Each model becomes easier to build and finish. The amount of time and effort decreases as the lessons learned with practice take effect.

Practice will work for you, too. Once you get rolling, you'll be able to turn out miniature masterpieces within a few days. It is important not to become discouraged by setbacks and backfires. Analyze the problem, work around it, and remember the solution. You'll be ready for it next time.

And your next model will look better than your last.

SOURCES

KITS FEATURED IN THIS BOOK

Airfix A-26 Invader: Humbrol Ltd., Marfleet, Kingston-upon-Hull HU9 5NE, England. Phone: 44-1428-701191

Czech Resin A-36A Apache: Aviation Usk, 602 Front St., Box 97, Usk, WA 99180. Phone: 509-445-1236

Eagles Talon Temco TT-1 Pinto: Eagles Talon, P.O. Box 295002, Lewisville, TX 75029

Ertl/Esci F-100D Super Saber: Ertl Company, P.O. Box 500, Dyersville, IA 52040-0500

Hasegawa F6F-5 Hellcat and FM-1 Wildcat: Marco Polo Import Inc., 532 S. Coralridge Place, City of Industry, CA 91746

Monogram F-117A Stealth Fighter and F11C-2 Goshawk: Revell/Monogram, 8601 Waukegan Road, Morton Grove, IL 60053-2295. Phone: 847-966-3500

TOOLS AND MATERIALS

Airwaves detail sets: E.D. Models, 64 Stratford Road, Shirley, Solihull, West Midlands B90-3LP, England

Brass tubing: K&S Engineering, 6917 W. 59th St., Chicago, IL 60638. Phone: 312-586-8503

Drafting tape and Scotch Tape: 3M

Elmer's Glue-All: Borden

Falcon canopies: available from Squadron Mail Order (see Line scriber, below)

FineScale Modeler magazine: Kalmbach Publishing Co., P.O. Box 1612, Waukesha, WI 53187. Phone: 414-796-8776

Future floor polish: S.C. Johnson & Son, Inc., Racine, WI 53403. Phone: 800-558-5252

Gundam markers: Marco Polo Import Inc., 532 S. Coralridge Place, City of Industry, CA 91746

In-Action and Detail & Scale books: Squadron/Signal Publications, 1115 Crowley Drive, Carrollton, TX 75011-5010. Phone: 972-242-8663

Light control circuit: Richmond Controls, P.O. Box 219095, Houston, TX 77218-9095

Line scriber: Squadron tools, Squadron Mail Order, 1115 Crowley Drive, Carrollton, TX 75011-5010. Phone: 972-242-8663

Liquid cement: Weld-On, Industrial Polychemical Service, P.O. Box 379, Gardena, CA 90247

Microbrush: Microbrush Corp., 1376 Cheyenne Ave., Grafton, WI 53024. Phone: 414-375-4011

Millennium 2000 polishing kit: MSC Model Products, 22 South Balsam St., Lakewood, CO 80226. Phone: 303-239-6559

Miniature light bulbs: Miniatronics, 561-K Acorn St., Deer Park, NY 11729. Phone: 800-942-9439

Miniature Motors: Edmund Scientific Co., 101 East Gloucester Pike, Barrington, NJ 08007-1380. Phone: 609-573-6250

Motor tool: Dremel, 4915 21st St., Racine, WI 53401-9989. Phone: 800-437-3635

Paintbrushes, drill bits, and other tools: Micro Mark, 340 Snyder Ave., Berkeley Heights, NJ 07922-1595. Phone: 908-464-6764

Parafilm M: Testor's (see under MODELING PAINTS)

TOOLS AND MATERIALS, CONT'D

Paragon resin conversions: Paragon Designs, Unit 10E, Folgate Road, North Walsham, Norfolk NR28 0AJ, England. Phone: 44-1692-407577

Parts nipper: Xuron Corp., 60 Industrial Park Road, Saco, ME 04072-1840. Phone: 207-283-1401

Pastel chalks: Grumbacher

Polly S Prep: Floquil-Polly S Color Corp. (see under MODELING PAINTS)

Razor saw: Zona Tool Co., P.O. Box 502, Bethel, CT 06801. Phone: 800-696-3480

Sanding pads: Flex-i-Pads, Creations Unlimited, 2011 Plainfield Ave. NE, Grand Rapids, MI 49505

Self-stick foil: Bare-Metal Foil Hobby Co., P.O. Box 82, Farmington, MI 48332. Phone: 810-476-4366

Sheet, rod, and tube styrene: Evergreen Scale Models, Inc., 12808 NE 125th Way, Kirkland, WA 98034

Spray booth: North Coast Prototype Models, 126 Second St., New Castle, DE 19720

Stainless-steel tubing: Accurate Detailing, 14859 E. Wagontrail Drive, Aurora, CO 80015. Phone: 303-699-1803

Super glue: Zap-a-Gap, Zip Kicker; Pacer Technology, 9420 Santa Anita Ave., Rancho Cucamonga, CA 91730

Tenax 7R: Hebco Inc., 306 Briar Hollow Rd., Hohenwald, TN 38462

True Details parts: Squadron Mail Order (see Line scriber, above)

X-acto knives, blades: Hunt Manufacturing Co., 2005 Market St., Philadelphia, PA 19103-7085

MODELING PAINTS

Floquil-Polly-S/Bondex International, 206 Milvan Drive, Weston, ON M9l 1Z9, Canada. Phone: 888-476-5597

SnJ Model Products, P.O. Box 292713, Sacramento, CA 95829. Phone: 916-428-7217

Tamiya America, 2 Orion, Aliso Viejo, CA 92656-4200. Phone: 800-826-4922

Testor's Corp., 620 Buckbee St., Rockford, IL 61104-4891. Phone: 815-962-6654

AIRBRUSHES

Badger Airbrush Co., 9128 W. Belmont Ave., Franklin Park, IL 60131. Phone: 800-247-2787

Binks Manufacturing, 9201 W. Belmont Ave., Franklin Park, IL 60131. Phone: 708-671-3000

Floquil (see under MODELING PAINTS)

Paasche Airbrush Company, 7440 W. Lawrence Ave., Harwood Heights, IL 60656-3497. Phone: 708-867-9191

ProModeler, Revell/Monogram, 8601 Waukegan Road, Morton Grove, IL 60053-2295. Phone: 847-966-3500

Testor's (see under MODELING PAINTS)

DECALS

AeroMaster Products, 3615 NW 20th Ave., Miami, FL 33142. Phone: 305-633-7398

Microscale Industries, 1570 Sunland Lane, Costa Mesa, CA 92626

Scale-Master Decals, available from Pacific Aero Press, P.O. Box 2643, Vista, CA 92085-2643. Phone: 619-724-5703

SuperScale International, P.O. Box 1017, Carson City, NV 89702

Three Guys Replicas, 817 Grand Ave., West Des Moines, IA 50265. Phone: 515-223-0034

DECAL-SETTING SOLUTIONS

AeroMaster (see under DECALS)

Floquil-Polly S Color Corp. (see under MODELING PAINTS)

Microscale (see under DECALS)

SuperScale International (see under DECALS)

Testor's (see under MODELING PAINTS)